KINGDOM CULTURE

Living as Citizens of Heaven on Earth

KINGDOM CULTURE

LIVING AS CITIZENS OF HEAVEN ON EARTH

TOM CORNELL

Paperback ISBN: 978-1-969882-33-3

CONTENTS

Introduction vii

1. Love Is the Highest Goal 1
2. Humility — The Posture of Heaven 9
3. Honor — Seeing People Through Heaven's Lens 17
4. Wholeness, Freedom, and Responsibility 25
5. Hosting the Presence of God 32
6. Living by the Word and the Voice of God 40
7. Kingdom Family — From Isolation to Covenant 46
8. Generosity — Living from Overflow 53
9. Unity — Protecting What God Blesses 59
10. Hunger — The Engine of Revival 66
11. Legacy — Building Beyond Yourself 73
12. Identity and Sonship 79
13. Kingdom Order and Authority 85
14. Spirit-Led Discipleship 91
15. Truth in Love — Kingdom Communication 97
16. Holiness and Hiddenness 104
17. Powerful People Who Fight for Connection 110

Conclusion 117
About the Author 123

INTRODUCTION

CULTURE ISN'T TAUGHT—IT'S CAUGHT

There is a difference between knowing the truth and living it. This may be one of the greatest tensions in the life of a believer. You can know what the Bible says. You can believe it is true. You can even defend it, teach it, and build your life around it externally—and still find yourself struggling internally to walk in the fullness of it.

Many believers today are not lacking information. They are surrounded by it. Sermons are more accessible than ever. Podcasts, books, teachings, conferences—truth is everywhere. Yet for many, transformation feels inconsistent, distant, or incomplete. They love God, but they wrestle. They believe in freedom, but they feel bound. They know they are called to walk in victory, but their experience doesn't always match the promise.

The issue is not always a lack of truth. The issue is often a lack of alignment with the culture of the Kingdom. Because while doctrine defines what we say we believe, culture reveals how we actually live. Doctrine can be learned quickly. Culture is formed slowly. Doctrine informs the mind, but culture shapes the instincts. It determines how you respond without thinking. It shows up in your reactions, your tone, your relationships, your priorities, and your patterns. It reveals itself not in what you declare in moments of strength, but in how you live in moments of pressure.

You can believe in love and still respond with offense.
You can believe in grace and still live under pressure.
You can believe in freedom and still live in cycles.
You can believe in identity and still strive for approval.

Why? Because belief alone does not change culture. Culture is not primarily taught—it is caught. It is absorbed through environment. It is reinforced through repetition. It is shaped by what you are surrounded by, what you are exposed to, and what you consistently participate in. It is formed by what is normalized, what is celebrated, and what is tolerated.

Every person, whether they realize it or not, is living from a culture. The real question is not whether you have one. The real question is whether it reflects Heaven. When Jesus came, He did not come simply to introduce a new set of beliefs. He came announcing a Kingdom. His message was not, "Here is a new religion." His message was, "Repent, for the Kingdom of Heaven is at hand."

That word repent is often misunderstood. It does not simply mean to feel bad or to turn away from sin, though it includes that. At its core, it means to change the way you think—to come into alignment with a new reality. Jesus was saying, "A new Kingdom has arrived, and if you are going to live in it, you must think differently."

Because you cannot enter a new Kingdom with an old mindset. You cannot live in a new reality while holding onto an old culture. The Kingdom of God is not just about eternity—it is about present reality. It is not just about where you are going—it is about how you are living now.

It is a different way of thinking, where truth is not just known but embodied. It is a different way of relating, where love is not conditional but covenantal. It is a different way of living, where identity is received, not achieved. It is a different way of building, where people matter more than platforms and presence matters more than performance.

The Kingdom is not just a message to be believed. It is a culture to be lived. The challenge is that we do not come into the Kingdom as blank slates.

Every person is shaped by something before they ever encounter Jesus. You are shaped by your upbringing, your family dynamics, your experiences, your wounds, your environment, and the world around you. You are discipled long before you realize you are being discipled.

The world is constantly forming culture. It teaches you how to respond when you are hurt. It teaches you how to define success. It teaches you how to view yourself and others. It teaches you how to handle conflict, pressure, and relationships. And the culture of the world is often in direct opposition to the culture of the Kingdom.

The world teaches self-promotion, but the Kingdom teaches humility. The world teaches independence, but the Kingdom teaches covenant. The world teaches offense, but the Kingdom teaches forgiveness. The world teaches scarcity, but the Kingdom teaches abundance. The world teaches performance, but the Kingdom teaches identity. The world teaches control, but the Kingdom teaches surrender.

If you are not intentional, you will default to the culture you were formed by instead of the culture you were saved into. Because salvation changes your spirit, but transformation renews your mind. And the renewing of the mind is not automatic—it is intentional. It is a process of unlearning one culture and learning another. It is the process of tearing down old patterns and building new ones. It is choosing, daily, to align your life with Heaven instead of drifting back into what is familiar.

Culture is not something you carry only in church settings. It is not something you turn on during worship or teaching moments. It is something that lives in you and flows through you in every area of your life.

It is the atmosphere you carry. You don't have to explain it—people feel it. They feel it in your home. They feel it in your conversations. They feel it in your leadership. They feel it in your response when things don't go your way. They feel it in how you treat people who can do nothing for you.

Culture is what remains when the moment is over. It is what you default to when you are tired, frustrated, or stretched. It is what shapes your reactions, not just your intentions. When Kingdom culture is present, something shifts.

There is a sense of safety that cannot be manufactured. People begin to open up, often without knowing why. Walls begin to come down. Freedom begins to happen naturally. Hunger for God increases. Relationships deepen. The presence of God becomes tangible—not because of a program, but because of an atmosphere that welcomes Him.

This is what Jesus carried. He did not just preach the Kingdom—He embodied it. Everywhere He went, the atmosphere changed. The sick were healed. The oppressed were delivered. The rejected were restored. The overlooked were seen. Not because He created events, but because He carried a culture.

He did not adjust to the environment—He transformed it. And now, through the Holy Spirit, that same life lives in us. Which means we are not just called to believe in the Kingdom—we are called to carry it. There is a difference between being a believer and being a culture carrier.

A believer agrees with truth. A culture carrier lives it. A believer receives. A culture carrier reproduces. A believer attends environments. A culture carrier creates them. A believer is shaped by what they encounter. A culture carrier shapes what they encounter. The Kingdom is not looking for people who simply agree with it—it is looking for people who embody it.

Culture carriers are people who have allowed the values of Heaven to shape their inner world so deeply that it naturally flows out into their external world. They do not need to force it. They do not need to perform it. It is who they have become.

When they walk into a room, love increases. Peace becomes tangible. Clarity replaces confusion. Hope rises. Freedom becomes possible. Not because they are trying to change the atmosphere, but because they are carrying a different one. They are not reacting to the world—they are revealing Heaven. This is why this book exists.

This is not just a book about principles. It is not just a collection of teachings. It is a call to alignment. It is a blueprint for how Heaven's people are meant to live. It is an invitation to move beyond knowing what is right and into living what is true.

Each chapter will walk through a core value of the Kingdom. Not just what it means, but what it looks like when it is lived out.

Because values are not meant to remain ideas—they are meant to become lifestyle.

You will see how love is not just something we talk about, but something that defines how we respond. How humility is not weakness, but the posture that attracts grace. How honor transforms relationships. How wholeness and freedom are not rare, but normal. How the presence of God is not occasional, but central. How hearing His voice is not reserved for a few, but available to all. How family is not convenience, but covenant. How generosity flows from identity. How unity must be protected. How hunger must be maintained.

This is not about perfection—it is about alignment. Transformation does not happen because you read something once. It happens as truth is embraced, practiced, and lived repeatedly until it becomes natural.

This book is meant to challenge you. It is meant to confront areas where your life may be out of alignment with the Kingdom. Not to condemn you, but to invite you higher. Not to burden you, but to free you.

Because the culture of the Kingdom is not restrictive—it is liberating. It is the way you were created to live. You were never meant to blend into the culture of the world. You were created to carry something different. To bring Heaven into your home. Into your marriage. Into your friendships. Into your workplace. Into your church. Into your city.

You were created to be a visible expression of an invisible Kingdom. When Kingdom culture is lived, everything changes. Families begin to heal. Relationships are restored. People encounter freedom. Churches become alive. Communities are impacted.

Not because of strategy alone, but because Heaven has found a people who will carry its ways. This is your invitation. An invitation to go beyond belief into transformation. An invitation to move beyond information into alignment. An invitation to live not just as a Christian, but as a citizen of Heaven.

To think differently.
To live differently.
To love differently.
To build differently.

To become someone who does not just visit the presence of God—but carries it. Someone who does not just talk about the Kingdom—but lives it. This is Kingdom culture. This is how Heaven's people live. And this is your invitation to live it.

1

LOVE IS THE HIGHEST GOAL

THE FOUNDATION OF EVERYTHING

If you misunderstand love, you will misunderstand the Kingdom.

This is not a small statement—it is a foundational one. Because everything in the Kingdom of God flows from love, is sustained by love, and ultimately returns to love. Love is not one value among many. It is not one principle alongside others. It is the foundation upon which every other Kingdom value stands.

The Kingdom does not function apart from love.

Many people try to live out spiritual principles without being rooted in love. They pursue truth without love. They pursue holiness without love. They pursue authority without love. And when love is missing, even what is right becomes distorted.

Truth without love becomes harsh.
Holiness without love becomes legalism.
Authority without love becomes control.
Correction without love becomes rejection.
Without love, the Kingdom is misrepresented.

This is why Scripture does not simply say that God has love or that God shows love—it declares that God is love. Love is not something God does occasionally. It is who He is eternally. It is His nature, His essence, His way of being.

Which means if we are going to live as His people, we must not just practice love—we must become people who are formed by it. You cannot represent a God you do not reflect. And if God is love, then love must become the foundation of everything in our lives.

More Than a Feeling—A Nature

One of the greatest misunderstandings about love is reducing it to a feeling.

The world defines love primarily as emotion—something you fall into, something you feel strongly, something that comes and goes depending on circumstances. But Kingdom love is not rooted in emotion. It is rooted in nature.

God does not love because He feels like it. He loves because it is who He is. That means His love is not conditional, not reactive, and not fragile. It does not rise and fall based on behavior. It is steady, consistent, and unchanging.

This is the love we are called into. Not a love that depends on how people treat us, but a love that flows from who we have become in Christ.

This is where many believers struggle. They are trying to love people from their own strength, their own emotions, and their own capacity. And when people disappoint them, offend them, or hurt them, their love runs out.

But Kingdom love is not sourced from your humanity—it is sourced from your union with God. When you abide in Him, His love flows through you.

This is why Jesus could love people who rejected Him, betrayed Him, and ultimately crucified Him. He was not drawing from human emotion—He was living from divine nature. And that same nature now lives in us.

Love as the Measure of Maturity

In the Kingdom, maturity is not measured by how much you know—it is measured by how well you love.

- You can know Scripture and still be immature.
- You can operate in gifts and still be immature.
- You can lead people and still be immature.

But you cannot walk in true love and remain immature. Love is the evidence of transformation.

This is where the Kingdom confronts much of what we celebrate. We often measure maturity by knowledge, platform, influence, or gifting. But Heaven measures differently.

Heaven measures by love.

- How do you treat people when they disappoint you?
- How do you respond when you are misunderstood?
- How do you handle conflict?
- How do you speak about others when they are not in the room?
- How do you love people who can give you nothing in return?

These are the measurements of maturity in the Kingdom. Because love is not proven in easy moments—it is revealed in difficult ones.

- Anyone can love when it is convenient.
- Anyone can love when it is reciprocated.
- Anyone can love when it feels good.

But Kingdom love is revealed when it costs you something. It is revealed when you choose patience instead of irritation. When you choose forgiveness instead of offense. When you choose kindness instead of retaliation. When you choose to stay committed when it would be easier to walk away. This is maturity. And this is what the Kingdom is forming in us.

Covenant Love vs Convenient Love

There is a type of love that the world practices, and there is a type of love that the Kingdom produces. The world practices convenient love.

Convenient love is based on preference. It is sustained by feelings. It continues as long as it is easy and beneficial. It says, "I will love you as long as this works for me." But the Kingdom operates in covenant love.

Covenant love is not based on preference—it is based on commitment. It is not sustained by emotion—it is sustained by identity. It does not ask, "Is this easy?" It asks, "Is this who I am?" Covenant love says, "I am not going anywhere."

This is the love God has toward us. He does not love us because we are always consistent—He loves us because He is consistent. His love is anchored in His nature, not our behavior.

And this is the love we are called to walk in. This kind of love transforms relationships. It creates safety. It builds trust. It allows people to grow without fear of being discarded. It produces depth instead of surface-level connection.

Where convenient love creates instability, covenant love creates strength. And if we are going to build Kingdom families, Kingdom friendships, and Kingdom communities, they must be built on covenant love—not convenience.

Love That Confronts and Covers

One of the tensions people feel with love is misunderstanding what it actually looks like in practice. Some people think love means avoiding conflict. Others think love means never confronting anything. But that is not Kingdom love—that is passive love, and passive love is not powerful.

Kingdom love is both tender and strong. It covers—but it also confronts. It restores—but it also corrects. It is patient—but it is also truthful. Love does not ignore what is destructive—it addresses it in a way that leads to life. Because love is not about avoiding discomfort—it is about pursuing transformation.

If you truly love someone, you will not leave them where they are if where they are is hurting them or others. But you will also not confront them in a way that shames or crushes them. Love confronts with the goal of restoration, not rejection.

It speaks truth, but it does so with honor. It addresses issues, but it protects identity. It calls people higher, but it walks with them in the process. This is how God loves us. And this is how we are called to love others.

Love as Spiritual Warfare

Many people think of spiritual warfare as something aggressive, intense, and external. But one of the most powerful forms of warfare in the Kingdom is love.

Love is not passive—it is powerful. Love breaks offense. Love disarms division. Love overcomes hatred. Love silences accusation. Love destroys the works of the enemy at their root. The enemy thrives in environments of offense, bitterness, division, and fear. But when love is present, those things lose their power.

Love is not weak—it is the strongest force in the Kingdom. It takes strength to forgive. It takes strength to remain patient. It takes strength to choose kindness when you have been wronged. It takes strength to love when it is not being returned.

This is warfare. Not reacting according to the flesh, but responding according to the Spirit. Not allowing darkness to dictate your behavior, but allowing love to define it. When you choose love, you are not just being kind—you are advancing the Kingdom.

Becoming People of Love

The goal is not just to practice love occasionally—the goal is to become people who are formed by it. This means allowing God to transform the way you think, the way you respond, and the way you see others.

It means letting Him deal with the areas of your heart where love has been hindered—wounds, offenses, fears, and disappointments that have caused you to close off or pull back. Because you cannot give what you have not allowed yourself to receive.

You must first experience the love of God deeply and personally. Not just as a concept, but as a reality. You must allow Him to love you in your weaknesses, in your struggles, and in your imperfections. Because when you are secure in His love, you stop striving for it elsewhere.

And when you stop striving for it, you become free to give it. Love begins to flow naturally—not because you are trying harder, but because you are living from a different place.

Living from Love, Not for Love

This may be one of the most important shifts you can make. Many people live trying to earn love. They perform for it. They strive for it. They adjust themselves to be accepted. But in the Kingdom, you do not live for love—you live from it. You are already loved. Fully. Completely. Without condition. And when you live from that place, everything changes.

You no longer need people to affirm you in order to feel secure. You no longer need to prove yourself. You no longer need to control outcomes. You are free. And from that freedom, love flows.

The Highest Goal

At the end of everything, love remains. Not your achievements. Not your platform. Not your success. Love. This is why it is the highest goal. Not just something to aim for—but something to build your entire life around. Because when love is the foundation, everything else aligns. And when love is absent, everything else eventually breaks down.

Love is not optional in the Kingdom. It is the standard. It is the foundation. It is the evidence. It is the weapon. It is the goal. This is Kingdom culture. And this is where it begins.

Reflection Questions

1. Do I measure my spiritual maturity by what I know and do, or by how consistently I love people—especially in difficult situations?
2. Where in my life have I been operating with conditional or convenient love instead of covenant love, and what would it look like to shift that?
3. How would my relationships, decisions, and daily interactions change if love truly became my highest goal and standard?

2

HUMILITY — THE POSTURE OF HEAVEN

THE DOORWAY TO THE KINGDOM

If love is the foundation of the Kingdom, humility is the posture that allows you to live in it.

You cannot carry the culture of Heaven without humility. It is not optional. It is not a personality trait for a few—it is the required posture for anyone who wants to walk with God, hear His voice, carry His presence, and be trusted with His authority. Humility is the doorway.

Many people want the promises of God, the power of God, and the authority of God—but they resist the posture that makes those things possible. They want elevation without surrender. They want influence without brokenness. They want to be seen without being formed.

But in the Kingdom, everything flows through humility. God does not build on pride. He does not entrust His weight to people who are not grounded in humility. Because pride cannot sustain what God releases. Humility is not just how you begin—it is how you continue.

Pride vs Humility in the Kingdom

To understand humility, you must first understand pride. Pride is not always loud or obvious. It is not just arrogance, self-promotion, or thinking highly of yourself. Those are expressions of pride, but pride itself runs deeper.

At its core, pride is independence from God. It is the belief that you can do life on your own terms. That you know best. That you do not need correction, accountability, or guidance. It resists surrender and avoids submission. It protects itself instead of opening itself.

Pride says	Humility says
"I've got this."	"I need Him."
Pride resists correction.	Humility welcomes it.
Pride defends itself.	Humility examines itself.
Pride seeks recognition.	Humility seeks alignment.
Pride compares.	Humility stays secure.
Pride wants to be right.	Humility wants to grow.

This is the contrast of the Kingdom. And the danger of pride is that it often hides behind strength, gifting, and success. You can be talented and prideful. You can be influential and prideful. You can even be spiritually active and prideful. But pride always leads to separation—from God, from people, and ultimately from purpose.

Because pride rejects the very things that would keep you aligned. Humility, on the other hand, keeps you connected. It keeps you teachable. It keeps you dependent. It keeps you open. It keeps you growing. And this is why humility is not weakness—it is strength under control.

Why Humility Attracts Grace and Authority

There is a principle in the Kingdom that cannot be ignored: God gives grace to the humble, but resists the proud. This means humility does not just position you—it attracts something. It attracts grace.

Grace is not just forgiveness—it is empowerment. It is the enabling presence of God that allows you to do what you could not do on your own. It is what strengthens you, sustains you, and carries you beyond your natural capacity. And grace flows toward humility. Why? Because humility creates space for God to move.

Pride	Humility
Pride fills the space with self.	Humility makes room for Him.
Pride relies on its own strength.	Humility depends on His strength.
Pride says, "I can handle this."	Humility says, "God, I need You."

And where there is dependence, there is access. This is also why humility is directly connected to authority. In the Kingdom, authority is not given to those who demand it—it is given to those who are trusted with it. And trust is built through humility.

Authority flows from submission. If you are not submitted, you cannot be trusted with authority. Because authority without humility becomes dangerous. It leads to control, manipulation, and misuse. But when someone is humble, they understand that authority is not about them—it is about stewardship.

They do not use it to elevate themselves. They use it to serve others. They do not protect their position. They protect people. They do not need to prove anything. They simply remain aligned. This is why the greatest authority in the Kingdom is carried by the most humble people.

Living Low to Be Lifted by God

One of the patterns you see throughout Scripture is that those who choose humility are the ones God chooses to lift. This is the paradox of the Kingdom. The way up is down. Not down in value, but down in posture.

Humility is choosing to live low—not thinking less of yourself, but thinking of yourself less. It is not self-rejection. It is self-alignment. It is understanding who you are in God, but not needing to prove it to others.

It is being secure enough to serve. Secure enough to wait. Secure enough to be overlooked. Secure enough to let God be the one who lifts you. Pride tries to elevate itself. Humility trusts God to elevate. And when God lifts you, it is different. It is sustainable. It is protected. It is aligned with purpose.

Self-promotion may get you somewhere quickly, but it cannot keep you there. Only God can sustain what He establishes. This is why humility is not about staying small—it is about staying aligned. Because when you are aligned, God can trust you with more. More influence. More responsibility. More impact. Not because you are striving for it, but because you are ready for it.

Humility in Leadership

Humility becomes most visible when you are given influence. It is easy to appear humble when you have nothing to lead. But leadership reveals what is actually in you. It exposes whether you are leading from identity or insecurity, from love or control, from humility or pride.

Humble leaders do not lead to be seen—they lead to serve.

They are not driven by position—they are driven by purpose. They do not need to be the center—they are focused on building others. A humble leader listens.

They do not assume they have all the answers. They create space for others to speak, to contribute, and to grow. They value input, not as a threat, but as an opportunity to see more clearly.

A humble leader is teachable. They remain open to correction, even when it is uncomfortable. They do not surround themselves with people who only affirm them—they welcome people who will challenge them with truth.

A humble leader takes responsibility. They do not shift blame or protect their image. They own their mistakes, learn from them, and grow through them. They understand that leadership is not about perfection—it is about integrity.

A humble leader empowers others. They are not threatened by the growth of others—they celebrate it. They do not need to control everything—they trust, delegate, and develop people.

This is Kingdom leadership. It is not about control—it is about cultivation.

Humility in Discipleship

Humility is not just for leaders—it is essential for disciples. You cannot grow if you are not humble. Growth requires correction. It requires adjustment. It requires the willingness to see what you cannot see on your own. And without humility, those things are resisted.

A humble disciple is teachable. They do not assume they already know. They remain open, hungry, and willing to learn.

They ask questions. They seek understanding. They do not just listen to respond—they listen to receive.

A humble disciple receives correction. They do not take it as rejection—they see it as refinement. They understand that correction is not meant to tear them down, but to build them up.

A humble disciple stays submitted. Not in a controlling or unhealthy way, but in a way that honors structure, leadership, and accountability. They understand that covering and guidance are protections, not restrictions.

A humble disciple stays hungry. They do not become complacent. They do not plateau. They continue to pursue growth, intimacy with God, and alignment with His ways. This is how transformation happens. Not through striving, but through surrender.

The Subtlety of Pride

One of the greatest dangers of pride is how subtle it can be. It can hide in comparison—measuring yourself against others. It can hide in offense—being easily hurt or defensive. It can hide in independence—avoiding accountability or correction. It can hide in insecurity—constantly needing affirmation or validation.

It can even hide in false humility—downplaying yourself while still being self-focused. Pride is not always loud—it is often quiet. But it always produces the same result: distance. Distance from God. Distance from people. Distance from growth. This is why humility must be intentional.

It is not something you drift into—it is something you choose. You choose to stay open. You choose to stay teachable. You choose to stay dependent. You choose to stay aligned.

Becoming a Person of Humility

Humility is not a moment—it is a lifestyle. It is formed over time as you consistently choose surrender over self, alignment over opinion, and dependence over independence. It is developed in the hidden places. In how you respond when no one sees. In how you handle correction. In how you treat people who cannot benefit you. In how you carry yourself when you are not recognized.

Humility is not about lowering your value—it is about aligning your life with truth. You are valuable. You are called. You are chosen. But you are also dependent. You are also being formed. You are also in process. And when you embrace that tension, you become someone God can trust.

The Posture That Sustains Everything

At the end of the day, humility is not just how you start with God—it is how you walk with Him. It is the posture that keeps you aligned. The posture that keeps you growing. The posture that keeps you protected. Without humility, what you build will eventually collapse. With humility, what God builds through you will last.

Humility is the posture of Heaven. It is how Heaven thinks. It is how Heaven leads. It is how Heaven relates. And if we are going to live as Heaven's people, we must carry Heaven's posture. This is Kingdom culture. And this is how we stay aligned with it.

Reflection Questions

1. In what areas of my life do I tend to rely on myself instead of depending on God, and what would it look like to walk in greater humility there?
2. How do I typically respond to correction, feedback, or being overlooked—and what does that reveal about pride or humility in my heart?
3. What would it look like for me to intentionally "live low" this week, choosing to serve, listen, and honor others without needing recognition?

3

HONOR — SEEING PEOPLE THROUGH HEAVEN'S LENS

THE CULTURE OF HEAVEN IS A CULTURE OF HONOR

If love is the foundation of the Kingdom and humility is the posture, then honor is the way we see people. Honor is not just a value in the Kingdom—it is a lens. It is how Heaven perceives people. It is how God relates to humanity. And if we are going to carry His culture, we must learn to see the way He sees.

Because the way you see people determines the way you treat them. If you see people through the lens of their flaws, you will relate to them with frustration. If you see people through the lens of their performance, you will relate to them with conditions. If you see people through the lens of your wounds, you will relate to them with distance.

But if you see people through Heaven's lens, you will relate to them with honor. Honor is the ability to recognize value in someone beyond their current behavior. It is seeing who they are created to be, not just who they are currently acting like. It is recognizing identity over performance. It is choosing to treat people according to their God-given worth, not their momentary expression.

This is how God sees us. He does not relate to us based on our worst moments—He relates to us based on our identity as sons and daughters. He sees the end from the beginning. He sees what He placed inside of us. He sees who we are becoming, even when we are still in process. And this is the lens we are invited into.

Honor Is Identity-Based, Not Performance-Based

One of the greatest shifts you must make in order to walk in Kingdom culture is moving from performance-based thinking to identity-based thinking.

The world operates on performance. You are valued based on what you do. You are accepted based on how you perform. You are celebrated when you succeed and often discarded when you fail. This creates a culture of pressure, comparison, and insecurity. But the Kingdom operates differently.

In the Kingdom, value is not earned—it is given. Every person carries inherent worth because they are created in the image of God. That worth does not fluctuate based on behavior. It does not increase when someone performs well or decrease when they fail. It is constant. Honor recognizes that.

Honor does not ignore behavior—but it refuses to define people by it. It says, "I see who you are, even if you are not fully living like it yet." This is not denial—it is vision. It is choosing to anchor your perspective in identity instead of being controlled by performance.

This is how Jesus interacted with people. He saw fishermen and called them leaders. He saw a tax collector and called him to follow. He saw a woman with a broken past and spoke to her dignity. He saw Peter in his instability and spoke to his future. He did not ignore their issues—but He did not reduce them to their issues. He honored their identity while calling them into transformation. And this is what honor does.

Calling Out the Gold

Honor is not passive—it is intentional. It does not just see value—it speaks to it. One of the most powerful expressions of honor is the ability to call out the gold in others. Gold represents what is valuable, what is hidden beneath the surface, what may not be immediately visible but is deeply real.

Every person has gold inside of them. But not everyone sees it. And many people have lived in environments where their flaws were highlighted more than their potential, where their mistakes were magnified more than their identity.

Honor changes that. Honor looks beyond the surface and begins to speak to what God has placed inside of someone. It calls out potential. It affirms identity. It strengthens what is good instead of only pointing out what is wrong.

This does not mean you ignore areas of growth—but it means you do not lead with them. Because people grow best in environments where they are seen, valued, and believed in. When you call out the gold in someone, you are partnering with Heaven's perspective.

You are reinforcing identity. You are building confidence. You are creating space for growth. And often, people will begin to rise to the level of what you see in them. Because honor does not just recognize value—it releases it.

Honor Protects Relationships

Where honor is present, relationships are protected. Where honor is absent, relationships begin to fracture. Honor creates safety. It allows people to be in process without fear of being rejected. It creates an environment where people can grow, learn, and even make mistakes without feeling like they will be discarded. This is essential for healthy relationships. Because no relationship can thrive without safety.

Honor protects how you speak to people. It protects how you speak about people. It protects how you handle conflict. It protects how you respond when you are hurt. It slows you down when emotions rise. It reminds you of who someone is, even when they are not acting like it. It keeps you from saying things you cannot take back.

Honor chooses to cover rather than expose. Not in a way that ignores sin or avoids truth, but in a way that protects dignity. It understands that correction should restore, not shame. That conversations should build, not destroy.

This is why honor is so critical in families, friendships, and leadership. Without honor, relationships become transactional. They are based on performance, convenience, or agreement. And when those things shift, the relationship weakens.

But with honor, relationships become covenantal. They are built on value, commitment, and identity. And those things create strength.

Honor Releases Growth

People do not grow in environments of dishonor. They may perform for a season, but they will not flourish. Dishonor creates insecurity. It causes people to shut down, to protect themselves, to withdraw. It makes people feel unseen, undervalued, and unsafe.

But honor creates the opposite. It creates confidence. It creates openness. It creates hunger for growth. When people feel honored, they are more willing to receive feedback. They are more open to correction. They are more motivated to grow—not out of pressure, but out of a desire to become who they are created to be.

Honor does not remove accountability—it strengthens it. Because when people know they are valued, they are more willing to take responsibility. This is why honor is not just relational—it is developmental.

It helps people become. It draws out potential. It strengthens identity. It accelerates growth. And this is what Kingdom culture is meant to do.

Dishonor as a Doorway to Division

If honor builds and protects, dishonor does the opposite. Dishonor is one of the most destructive forces in any environment. It erodes trust. It creates distance. It opens the door to offense, bitterness, and division.

Dishonor does not always look aggressive. Sometimes it is subtle. It can show up in how you speak about someone when they are not present. It can show up in sarcasm, criticism, or a lack of value. It can show up in comparison, competition, or judgment. It can show up in withdrawing, shutting down, or disengaging.

But regardless of how it appears, the result is the same. It separates. It separates people from each other. It separates people from leadership. It separates people from purpose. Dishonor shifts your focus from value to flaws. It causes you to fixate on what is wrong instead of what is right. It distorts your perspective and begins to justify distance. And once dishonor takes root, division is not far behind.

This is why dishonor must be confronted quickly—not just externally, but internally. You must guard your heart. Because dishonor often begins in thoughts before it ever shows up in words or actions.

Guarding a Heart of Honor

Honor is not automatic—it is intentional. You must choose it. You choose how you see people. You choose how you think about them. You choose how you speak to and about them. You choose how you respond when they hurt you. This requires maturity.

Because people will give you opportunities to be dishonoring. They will disappoint you. They will misunderstand you. They will fall short. But honor is not based on their behavior—it is based on your identity. You honor because of who you are, not because of what they do. This does not mean you ignore boundaries. It does not mean you tolerate dysfunction. But it does mean you refuse to let dishonor take root in your heart.

You can set boundaries and still honor. You can confront and still honor. You can create distance and still honor. Honor is not agreement—it is perspective.

Seeing Through Heaven's Lens

At the core of honor is vision. It is the ability to see people the way God sees them. Not just who they are—but who they are becoming. This requires you to slow down, to look deeper, and to resist the temptation to judge quickly. It requires you to move beyond surface-level perception and into spiritual discernment.

Because Heaven is not reacting to people's behavior—it is calling them into their identity. And when you begin to see people this way, everything changes. You become more patient. More compassionate. More hopeful. You stop writing people off. You stop reducing them to their mistakes. You start partnering with what God is doing in their life. This is honor.

Becoming a Culture of Honor

The goal is not just for individuals to walk in honor—the goal is for communities to be built on it. A culture of honor transforms everything. It changes how people interact. It changes how leaders lead. It changes how conflict is handled. It changes how growth happens.

It creates environments where people feel safe, valued, and empowered. And when people feel that, they thrive. This is what Heaven looks like. A place where people are seen, known, and valued. A place where identity is affirmed. A place where growth is supported. A place where love and humility are expressed through honor.

Honor is not optional in the Kingdom. It is essential. It is how we see. It is how we relate. It is how we build. This is Kingdom culture. And this is how Heaven's people see.

Reflection Questions

1. Do I tend to see people based on their behavior, or do I intentionally look for their God-given identity and potential?
2. When I speak about others—especially when they're not present—am I building them up with honor or allowing subtle dishonor to take root in my words?
3. Who in my life can I intentionally "call out the gold" in this week, and what would it look like to affirm their identity and value out loud?

4

WHOLENESS, FREEDOM, AND RESPONSIBILITY

MORE THAN SALVATION — THE CALL TO TRANSFORMATION

Salvation is the beginning, not the end. This is one of the most important truths a believer must understand if they are going to walk in the fullness of the Kingdom. Many people have encountered God enough to be saved, but not enough to be transformed. They have experienced forgiveness, but not freedom. They have received new life in their spirit, but their soul—mind, emotions, and will—remains shaped by old patterns, wounds, and mindsets.

And because of this, there is often a disconnect between what they believe and how they live. They love God, but they still struggle with fear. They know truth, but they still think in lies. They want to move forward, but they feel stuck in cycles. The issue is not salvation—it is transformation.

Salvation is instantaneous. It is a gift. It is the work of Jesus that brings you into right relationship with God. But transformation is a process. It is the ongoing work of the Holy Spirit renewing your mind, healing your heart, and aligning your life with truth.

You are saved in a moment—but you are transformed over time. And if you do not understand this, you will either become frustrated with yourself or settle for less than what God has made available. Because the Kingdom is not just about getting to Heaven—it is about becoming whole.

God's Desire Is Wholeness

God is not just interested in your eternity—He is interested in your wholeness. He cares about your spirit, your soul, and your body. He cares about your thoughts, your emotions, your memories, and your patterns. He cares about the hidden places of your life—the places no one else sees, the places where pain has shaped you, the places where lies have taken root.

Because what is hidden will eventually shape what is visible. You can only live out of what is happening within you. If your inner world is fractured, your outer world will reflect it. If your inner world is bound, your life will feel limited. But if your inner world is whole, your life will begin to flow with freedom.

This is why Jesus did not just preach forgiveness—He healed the broken, delivered the oppressed, and restored what was lost. Wholeness is not optional in the Kingdom—it is normal.

Inner Healing and Deliverance as Kingdom Normal

There has been a tendency in many places to treat inner healing and deliverance as something extreme, rare, or only for certain people. But when you look at the life and ministry of Jesus, you see something very different.

He consistently healed hearts. He consistently set people free. He consistently confronted what was binding people internally and spiritually. This was not a side ministry—it was central.

Because you cannot fully walk in freedom if you are still bound internally or spiritually.

Inner healing addresses the wounds of the soul—the pain, trauma, rejection, fear, and lies that shape how you think and feel. Deliverance addresses the spiritual influences that attach to those wounds and reinforce bondage.

These two often work together. Wounds create openings. Lies create agreement. And where there is agreement, the enemy finds access. But when healing happens and truth replaces lies, those doors close. This is why freedom must go deeper than behavior—it must reach the root.

You cannot simply manage symptoms. You must address the source. And this is what makes the Kingdom so powerful—it does not just modify behavior, it transforms the heart.

Freedom Is a Lifestyle, Not a Moment

Many people have experienced moments of freedom—but have not learned how to live free. They have encountered God powerfully. They have had moments where something broke, where something lifted, where something shifted. But over time, they find themselves slipping back into old patterns.

Why? Because freedom is not sustained by a moment—it is sustained by a lifestyle. Freedom requires maintenance. Not in a burdensome way, but in an intentional way. You must guard what God has done. You must steward your mind. You must remain aligned with truth. Because the enemy often returns to see if what was once broken is still guarded.

If old thought patterns return and are not resisted, they can reestablish strongholds. If old agreements are revisited, doors can reopen. This is why Scripture speaks about renewing the mind. Freedom is not just something that happens to you—it is something you walk in.

It is choosing truth daily. It is rejecting lies quickly. It is staying aware of what is influencing your thoughts, your emotions, and your decisions. Freedom is not passive—it is intentional.

Renewing the Mind

One of the primary ways transformation happens is through the renewing of the mind. Your mind is the gateway to your life. What you believe shapes how you think. How you think shapes how you feel. How you feel shapes how you act.

If your thinking is not aligned with truth, your life will not be aligned with truth. This is why transformation requires more than encounters—it requires renewal. You must replace lies with truth. If you believe you are unworthy, you will live from insecurity. If you believe you are rejected, you will expect abandonment. If you believe you are alone, you will isolate.

But when truth replaces those lies, everything shifts. You begin to live from identity instead of insecurity. You begin to relate from confidence instead of fear. You begin to walk in freedom instead of limitation. This is not automatic—it is intentional. You must take ownership of your thought life.

Responsibility as the Fruit of Maturity

One of the clearest signs of maturity in the Kingdom is responsibility. Immaturity avoids responsibility. Maturity embraces it. Immaturity blames others. Maturity takes ownership.

Immaturity makes excuses. Maturity makes adjustments. This is not about condemnation—it is about empowerment.

You cannot change what you do not take responsibility for. As long as everything is someone else's fault, you remain stuck. But the moment you take ownership, you step into authority. Responsibility says, "I may not have caused everything that happened to me, but I am responsible for how I respond to it."

This is where freedom grows. Because responsibility puts you back in a position to choose. To choose truth. To choose healing. To choose alignment. And this is what maturity looks like.

The Balance of Grace and Responsibility

There is a tension in the Kingdom between grace and responsibility. Grace is what God gives you. Responsibility is what you do with it. Grace empowers you—but it does not replace your participation. God will heal—but you must engage. God will speak—but you must listen. God will lead—but you must follow.

Transformation is not passive—it is cooperative. You work with what God is doing. This is where many people get stuck. They either lean too far into grace and become passive, waiting for God to do everything, or they lean too far into effort and begin striving. But the Kingdom is both. You receive—and you respond. You are empowered—and you engage.

Becoming Whole

Wholeness is not perfection. It is integration. It is your spirit, soul, and body coming into alignment with truth. It is no longer being fragmented by wounds, lies, and conflicting patterns. It is becoming consistent, stable, and free.

It does not mean you never struggle—it means you are no longer controlled. It means you are aware, responsive, and aligned. It means when something surfaces, you address it. You bring it into the light. You invite God into it. You do not ignore it, suppress it, or avoid it. Wholeness is a journey—but it is a real one. And it is available.

Living Free

Freedom is not just something you receive—it is something you live. It shows up in how you think. How you respond. How you relate. How you make decisions. It shows up in peace instead of anxiety. In confidence instead of insecurity. In clarity instead of confusion. It is not the absence of challenge—it is the presence of alignment. And when you live from that place, everything changes.

A Culture of Wholeness

The goal is not just for individuals to be whole—the goal is for communities to be whole. Where wholeness is normal, people grow. Where freedom is normal, people thrive. Where responsibility is embraced, maturity develops.

This is what Kingdom culture produces. Not perfection—but transformation. Wholeness is the goal. Freedom is the lifestyle. Responsibility is the evidence. This is Kingdom culture. And this is what it looks like within the life of the believer.

Reflection Questions

1. In what areas of my life am I saved but not yet fully transformed, and what might God be inviting me to heal or address at the root?
2. Do I treat freedom as a one-time experience or a daily lifestyle, and what patterns or thoughts do I need to actively guard or renew?
3. Where have I been avoiding responsibility for my growth, and what would it look like to take ownership and partner with God in my transformation?

5

HOSTING THE PRESENCE OF GOD

GOD'S DESIRE HAS ALWAYS BEEN TO DWELL

From the very beginning, God's desire has never been distant relationship—it has always been nearness. Before there were systems, structures, or gatherings, there was a garden. And in that garden, God walked with man. There was no separation, no striving, no performance—just presence. Humanity was not created merely to believe in God, but to live with Him, to walk with Him, to host Him. That was the original design, and everything since then has been about restoring that reality.

The story of Scripture is not simply about redemption—it is about restoration. It is about God bringing humanity back into proximity with Himself. You see it in the tabernacle, where His presence dwelt among His people. You see it in the temple, where His glory filled a physical space. And then you see it fulfilled in Jesus, where God Himself stepped into humanity and walked among us. But even that was not the final expression. Through the finished work of Jesus and the gift of the Holy Spirit, God no longer dwells in buildings made by human hands—He dwells in people.

This changes everything. You were not created to visit the

presence of God. You were created to carry it. You were not designed to have occasional encounters—you were designed to be a dwelling place. This is not symbolic language meant to inspire you. It is a spiritual reality meant to define you. The presence of God is not something external that you reach for—it is something internal that you learn to live aware of. And when this becomes real to you, your entire understanding of the Christian life begins to shift.

Presence Over Performance

One of the greatest obstacles to living in God's presence is the mindset of performance. Performance is subtle, but it is deeply ingrained in how many people relate to God. It tells you that closeness must be earned, that access must be maintained through effort, and that your consistency determines your connection. But presence operates differently.

Presence is not something you achieve—it is something you receive. It is not based on how well you perform—it is based on what Jesus has already accomplished. The veil has been torn. Access has been granted. God is not distant, waiting for you to reach Him—He is near, inviting you to become aware of Him.

This does not eliminate discipline, but it transforms the reason behind it. You are not praying to get God's attention—you are praying because you have it. You are not worshiping to bring Him near—He is already near. You are responding to presence, not striving to create it.

When you live from performance, your relationship with God becomes exhausting. You measure yourself constantly. You feel close on good days and distant on bad ones. But when you live from presence, your relationship becomes steady. You begin to realize that He is not coming and going—He is remaining. The shift from performance to presence is the shift from striving to abiding.

Learning to Abide

Abiding is not complicated, but it is deeply transformative. It is the simple, ongoing awareness that God is with you, in you, and near you at all times. It is not about intensity—it is about consistency. It is not about creating moments—it is about recognizing reality.

Most believers do not struggle with access to God's presence—they struggle with awareness of it. They are connected, but they are not conscious. They have the Spirit, but they are not attentive to Him. And because of this, they move through their day disconnected in experience even though they are connected in truth.

Abiding is learning to stay aware. It is turning your attention toward Him in the middle of ordinary moments. It is acknowledging Him while you are working, while you are driving, while you are in conversation. It is not about withdrawing from life—it is about including Him in it.

This awareness changes everything. It slows you down internally. It anchors you. It reminds you that you are not alone, not responsible to carry everything on your own, not left to navigate life without Him.

The more you practice this, the more natural it becomes. What once felt intentional begins to feel instinctive. You begin to live with a quiet awareness that He is always there.

Becoming a Dwelling Place

There is a difference between hosting God occasionally and becoming a place where He dwells. Many people have learned how to create environments where they encounter God. They know how to worship, how to pray, how to position themselves for a moment. But those moments often feel separate from the rest of their life. They encounter Him in certain spaces, but not in others.

Becoming a dwelling place changes that. It means your life becomes the environment where God is welcome. Not just in spiritual moments, but in every moment. It means you begin to carry an awareness of Him into your thoughts, your decisions, your relationships, and your daily rhythms.

This affects how you live. You begin to guard your inner world differently. You become more aware of what you allow your mind to dwell on. You become more sensitive to what disrupts peace, what pulls you out of alignment, what dulls your awareness. Not out of fear, but out of love.

Because when you value His presence, you begin to protect it. You begin to recognize that His presence is not just something you enjoy—it is something you carry. And when you carry something valuable, you steward it differently.

Sensitivity to the Spirit

The Holy Spirit is not loud or forceful. He is gentle. He leads, He nudges, He speaks—but He does not compete with noise. This is why sensitivity is so important. Sensitivity is not about trying harder to hear God—it is about removing what distracts you from recognizing Him.

Life is full of noise. Not just external noise, but internal noise. Thoughts, worries, distractions, constant input—these things can crowd your awareness and make it difficult to recognize what God is doing. But when you begin to slow down internally, something shifts.

You begin to notice what you didn't notice before. You begin to recognize His peace, His prompting, His voice. You become more aware of what aligns with Him and what does not. This is not reserved for a few—it is available to anyone willing to create space. And the more you respond to His leading, the more familiar His voice becomes.

Living Presence-Centered

Many believers have been trained to live event-centered lives. They encounter God in gatherings, in moments, in environments that are designed to facilitate His presence. And those moments are real and powerful—but they are not meant to be the only place you experience Him. A presence-centered life is different.

It does not depend on moments—it carries awareness. It does not wait for encounters—it lives connected. It does not rise and fall based on experiences—it remains anchored. This does not diminish the importance of gatherings—it puts them in their proper place. They are meant to reinforce what you are already living, not replace it.

You were never meant to live from encounter to encounter. You were meant to live from presence. And when you begin to live this way, your life becomes consistent. Your peace is not dependent on your environment. Your connection is not dependent on a moment. You carry something steady, something real.

Carrying His Presence

When you live aware of God's presence, you begin to carry it into every environment you step into. You are no longer just entering spaces—you are influencing them. This is not about trying to change atmospheres—it is about carrying one.

When you walk into a room, you bring peace. When you speak, there is weight. When you interact with people, something shifts. Not because you are trying to make something happen, but because you are carrying someone. The presence of God is not meant to stay contained within you—it is meant to flow through you. It impacts people, often without explanation. It creates space for freedom, for clarity, for hope.

And many times, people will encounter God through your life without even realizing why. Because presence is not always announced—it is felt.

Guarding What You Carry

When you begin to value God's presence, you begin to guard it. Not in a rigid or fearful way, but in a relational way. You become aware of what affects your sensitivity. You notice when your peace is disrupted. You recognize when your focus shifts away from Him. And instead of ignoring it, you respond to it.

You choose alignment. You choose to return your attention. You choose to let go of what is distracting. You choose to come back into awareness. This is not about perfection—it is about responsiveness. Because hosting His presence is not about never drifting—it is about returning quickly.

Union, Not Visitation

At the core of everything is this truth: you were not created for visitation—you were created for union. God does not want to visit your life occasionally—He wants to be integrated into it fully. He wants to walk with you, lead you, speak to you, and live through you.

This is the life Jesus modeled. He did not step in and out of connection with the Father—He lived in constant awareness of Him. Everything He did flowed from that connection. And now, through the Spirit, that same reality is available to you.

Not just moments—but a lifestyle. Not just encounters—but union. Not just awareness in certain places—but awareness in every place.

A Life That Hosts Him

When you begin to live this way, your life becomes something different. It becomes a place where God is welcome. A place where He is recognized. A place where He is responded to. And from that place, everything else flows. Your decisions become clearer. Your relationships become healthier. Your leadership becomes more effective. Your life becomes more aligned. Not because you are trying harder—but because you are living connected.

You were created to host Him. To walk with Him. To live aware of Him. Not occasionally—but continually. This is Kingdom culture. And this is what it means to live in His presence.

Reflection Questions

1. Do I relate to God primarily through performance or through presence, and what would it look like to shift into a deeper awareness of His nearness daily?
2. In what areas of my life am I only experiencing God in moments instead of carrying His presence as a lifestyle?
3. What practical changes can I make this week to become more aware of and responsive to God's presence throughout my day?

6

LIVING BY THE WORD AND THE VOICE OF GOD

A LIFE THAT IS LED, NOT JUST LIVED

The Kingdom life is not meant to be self-directed—it is meant to be God-led. This is one of the defining distinctions between simply believing in God and actually walking with Him. Many people believe in God, honor Scripture, and desire to live rightly, but they are still primarily making decisions based on their own understanding, their own reasoning, and their own perspective.

But the Kingdom invites you into something deeper. Not just a life informed by truth, but a life led by God. You were never meant to navigate your life alone. You were not designed to figure everything out through logic, experience, or trial and error. You were created to live in relationship with a God who speaks, who leads, who directs, and who desires to be involved in every area of your life.

This is what separates religion from relationship. Religion gives you principles. Relationship gives you guidance. Religion tells you what is right. Relationship leads you into what God is doing now. The Kingdom is not just about knowing what God has said—it is about hearing what He is saying.

The Word of God as Foundation

Before you can live led by the voice of God, you must be anchored in the Word of God. The written Word—Scripture—is the foundation of everything.

It is not optional. It is not secondary. It is the standard, the filter, and the anchor for your life. It reveals the nature of God, the character of God, the ways of God, and the truth of God. It establishes what is right, what is true, and what is aligned with His Kingdom.

Without the Word, you have no foundation. And without a foundation, you become vulnerable to confusion, deception, and instability. The Word grounds you. It shapes your thinking. It renews your mind. It aligns your perspective.

It gives you the framework through which you interpret life. But the Word is not just meant to be studied—it is meant to be lived. It is not just information—it is transformation.

And when you begin to build your life on it, something becomes stable within you. You are no longer tossed by circumstances or emotions. You are anchored in truth.

Logos and Rhema

Within Scripture, there is both the written Word and the spoken Word. The written Word is often referred to as logos. It is the established, revealed truth of God that has been given to all believers. It is consistent, unchanging, and foundational.

The spoken Word is often referred to as rhema. It is the living, present communication of God to you in a specific moment. It is not separate from Scripture—it is an extension of it. It is God speaking personally, specifically, and presently into your life.

You need both. Logos gives you the foundation. Rhema gives you direction. Logos tells you who God is. Rhema shows you what He is saying now. Logos establishes truth. Rhema applies it. If you have logos without rhema, your life can become rigid and informational. You know truth, but you lack personal guidance. If you have rhema without logos, your life can become unstable and subjective. You feel led, but you lack grounding.

But when the two come together, something powerful happens. You become both anchored and led.

The Spirit as Guide

Jesus said that the Spirit would lead us into all truth. This means you are not just left with a book—you are given a guide. The Holy Spirit is not silent. He speaks, He leads, He prompts, He reveals. He brings Scripture to life. He highlights truth in moments. He directs your steps. He gives you insight, wisdom, and discernment.

This is not reserved for a few—it is normal Christianity. The same Spirit that raised Jesus from the dead now lives in you. The same Spirit that spoke to prophets, led Jesus, and directed the early Church is now within you. And He desires to lead you. In your decisions. In your relationships. In your calling. In your daily life. But you must learn to recognize His voice.

Hearing God as Normal

For many people, hearing God feels distant, unclear, or reserved for a few. But the truth is, God is speaking. The question is not whether He is speaking—it is whether you are listening.

Hearing God is not always dramatic. It is often simple, quiet, and internal. It can come as a thought, a prompting, a sense, a Scripture that comes alive, or a deep inner knowing.

It is not always audible—but it is real. And the more you learn to recognize it, the more confident you become. This requires practice. You must slow down. You must create space. You must learn to discern. Because not every thought is from God—but His voice becomes familiar over time.

He will never contradict His Word. He will lead you into truth. He will produce peace, not confusion. And as you respond to His voice, your sensitivity increases.

Obedience Is the Proof

Hearing God is not the goal—obedience is. You can hear clearly and still remain unchanged if you do not respond. In the Kingdom, obedience is the evidence of relationship. It is the proof that you are not just listening, but following. And obedience is not always convenient. It will stretch you. It will challenge you. It will require trust.

Sometimes it will not make sense in the natural. Sometimes it will go against your preferences, your comfort, or your timing. But obedience is where transformation happens. Because every time you obey, something is formed in you. Trust grows. Faith strengthens. Alignment deepens. And over time, your life begins to reflect the voice you are following.

The Cost and Reward of Obedience

There is always a cost to obedience—but there is always a greater reward. The cost may be comfort. It may be control. It may be familiarity. But the reward is alignment with God. And alignment produces life.

Peace. Clarity. Fruitfulness. Impact. Because when you follow His voice, you step into what He is doing. And there is no safer place to be than in alignment with Him.

A Life Built on His Voice

The goal is not just to hear God occasionally—the goal is to build your life on His voice. To become someone who is consistently led. Consistently aware. Consistently responsive. Not perfect—but aligned. Where your decisions are shaped by Him. Your direction is guided by Him. Your life reflects Him.

You were not created to guess your way through life. You were created to be led. By His Word. By His Spirit. By His voice. This is Kingdom culture. And this is what it means to live led.

Reflection Questions

1. Am I building my life more on my own understanding or on God's Word and His voice, and where do I need greater alignment?
2. How consistently am I creating space to hear from God personally, and what might be distracting or dulling my sensitivity to His voice?
3. When God speaks or reveals truth to me, do I respond with obedience, or do I delay—and what step of obedience is He asking me to take right now?

7

KINGDOM FAMILY — FROM ISOLATION TO COVENANT

GOD IS BUILDING A FAMILY, NOT JUST A CHURCH

One of the greatest misunderstandings in modern Christianity is what the Church actually is. For many, the Church has been reduced to a place you attend, a service you participate in, or an organization you belong to. It is often viewed through the lens of structure, programming, and function. People think of buildings, gatherings, leadership roles, and systems. And while those things have a place, they are not the essence.

The Church was never meant to be an institution—it was always meant to be a family. This is not just a helpful metaphor. It is the design of God. From the beginning, God has revealed Himself as a Father. Not a distant ruler, not an abstract force, but a Father who desires sons and daughters. Salvation is not just about forgiveness—it is about adoption. It is about being brought into a family, into relationship, into belonging.

This changes how you see everything. You are not just saved from something—you are brought into something. You are not just forgiven—you are adopted. You are not just attending—you are belonging. The Kingdom is a family. And if you misunderstand that, you will try to live the Christian life in isolation or through shallow connection, and you will miss the depth of what God intended.

From Isolation to Belonging

Many people live in isolation, even when they are surrounded by others. They attend services but remain disconnected. They are present physically, but not known relationally. They may serve, give, and participate, but still feel alone beneath the surface.

This is one of the greatest struggles of our time. Because isolation is not just a physical condition—it is a relational and internal one. You can be in a crowd and still feel alone. You can be part of something and still feel like you don't belong.

But the Kingdom addresses this. Because belonging is not something you earn—it is something you receive. You belong because you are a son or daughter. And from that identity, you are invited into real relationship with others who share that same identity. This is what family provides.

A place where you are known. A place where you are seen. A place where you are valued beyond your function. Belonging is different than attending. Attending is participation. Belonging is connection. Attending is showing up. Belonging is being known. Attending can remain surface-level. Belonging requires vulnerability. And this is where many people hesitate. Because belonging costs something. It requires openness. It requires trust. It requires letting people see you beyond your strengths. But it is also where transformation happens. Because you cannot grow fully in isolation.

Covenant vs Convenience

The difference between worldly relationships and Kingdom

relationships often comes down to this: covenant versus convenience. Convenience says, "I will stay as long as this works for me." Covenant says, "I am committed, even when it costs me."

Convenience is based on preference. Covenant is based on commitment. Convenience disconnects when things get hard. Covenant leans in when things get difficult.

Many people approach relationships with a convenience mindset. They stay connected as long as it is easy, beneficial, and comfortable. But the moment there is conflict, tension, or discomfort, they pull back, disconnect, or move on. This is not Kingdom culture. The Kingdom is built on covenant.

Covenant says, "I am not here because everything is perfect—I am here because I am committed." This does not mean you ignore unhealthy situations or stay in dysfunction. But it does mean you do not treat relationships as disposable.

You work through things. You pursue reconciliation. You choose to stay engaged. Because covenant creates depth. And depth creates strength. This is how families are built.

The Role of Spiritual Family

In the natural, family is where identity is formed, values are passed down, and growth is nurtured. The same is true in the Kingdom. Spiritual family is where you are discipled, developed, and matured. It is where you are encouraged and corrected. Where you are supported and challenged. Where you are celebrated and refined.

This requires real relationship. Not just casual connection, but intentional investment. Because family is not built accidentally—it is built intentionally. It is built through time, through shared experiences, through walking with one another in both strength and weakness. And this is where many people must shift their mindset. The Church is not a place you consume—it is a family you contribute to. You are not just there to receive—you are there to build.

Spiritual Fathers and Mothers

One of the ways God expresses His heart in the Kingdom is through spiritual fathers and mothers. This is often misunderstood, but it is deeply biblical and deeply relational. Spiritual fathers and mothers are not about control—they are about care. They are not about hierarchy—they are about responsibility. They are people who take ownership of others' growth, who invest in them, guide them, and walk with them.

They provide:

- Identity — reminding you of who you are
- Direction — helping you navigate your path
- Correction — aligning you when you drift
- Covering — standing with you in both challenge and calling

This is not about replacing your relationship with God—it is about reinforcing it. God uses people to help shape people. And just as in the natural, maturity often comes through relationship with those who have gone before you. But this also requires humility and trust.

You must be willing to receive. Willing to be guided. Willing to be corrected. Because independence will limit your growth.

Generational Thinking

Kingdom family is not just about the present—it is about

legacy. God does not think in terms of moments—He thinks in terms of generations. He desires to see sons and daughters raised who become fathers and mothers, who then raise others, creating a multiplication of life, truth, and culture.

This is how the Kingdom expands. Not just through events or programs, but through people who reproduce what they have received. Generational thinking shifts your focus. You begin to think beyond yourself. Beyond your own growth. Into how you can invest in others.

Because maturity is not just about what you receive—it is about what you reproduce. And this is where family becomes powerful. It becomes a place of multiplication.

Healing the Fear of Family

For many people, the idea of family is complicated. They have experienced brokenness, dysfunction, or pain in natural family relationships. And because of that, they approach spiritual family with hesitation, guardedness, or mistrust.

This is real—and it must be acknowledged. But it must also be healed. Because if you allow past pain to define your expectations, you will limit your ability to experience what God intended. Kingdom family is not perfect—but it is designed to be healthy.

And as you walk in love, humility, honor, and wholeness, you begin to experience a different kind of relationship. One that restores what was broken, one that brings healing where there was pain. This is part of God's design. Not just to save you—but to restore your understanding of family.

Building a Culture of Family

Family does not happen automatically—it must be cultivated. It is built through intentional connection. Through creating space for real relationships. Through choosing to engage beyond surface-level interaction.

It is built through:

- Consistency — showing up
- Vulnerability — being real
- Commitment — staying connected
- Honor — valuing one another
- Love — covering and strengthening

When these things are present, something powerful begins to form. People begin to feel safe. They begin to open up. They begin to grow. And over time, what was once a group becomes a family.

You Were Not Meant to Do Life Alone

At the core of this chapter is a simple truth: You were not created to do life alone. Isolation may feel safe, but it is limiting. It protects you from pain, but it also prevents growth. It keeps you from being hurt, but it also keeps you from being known. The Kingdom invites you out of isolation and into covenant.

Into relationship. Into connection. Into family. This is where you are strengthened. This is where you are formed. This is where you become who you are called to be. God is not building an institution. He is building a family. And you are not just invited to attend—you are invited to belong. This is Kingdom culture. And this is how Heaven functions in relationships.

Reflection Questions

1. Am I truly living in Kingdom family, or am I mostly attending without deep connection—and what would it take for me to step into real belonging?
2. Do I approach relationships with a covenant mindset or a convenience mindset, especially when things become difficult or uncomfortable?
3. Who am I intentionally investing in or allowing to invest in me, and how am I participating in building generational legacy through spiritual family?

8

GENEROSITY — LIVING FROM OVERFLOW

GOD IS A GIVER BY NATURE

If you misunderstand generosity, you will misunderstand God. Because generosity is not just something God does—it is who He is. From the very beginning, God reveals Himself as a giver. He creates and then gives. He forms the earth and then gives it to humanity. He breathes life and gives it freely. He establishes provision before there is ever a need. Everything about Him flows outward, not inward.

God does not operate from lack—He operates from abundance. He does not give sparingly—He gives generously. He does not give reluctantly—He gives willingly. He does not give conditionally—He gives from His nature. This is most clearly seen in Jesus.

God did not give something small—He gave His Son. He gave what was most valuable, most costly, most significant. Not because humanity earned it, but because that is who He is. Which means if we are going to live as His people, generosity must become part of our nature as well. You cannot reflect a generous God while living a guarded life.

Living from Overflow, Not Emptiness

Many people approach generosity from the wrong starting point. They give out of pressure instead of overflow. They give out of obligation instead of identity. They give while feeling empty instead of full. And because of that, generosity feels difficult. But Kingdom generosity does not flow from emptiness—it flows from overflow.

You cannot give what you do not believe you have. And this is where identity matters. If you see yourself as lacking, you will hold tightly. If you see yourself as provided for, you will live openhanded. Generosity is not first about what you have—it is about what you believe.

- Do you believe that God is your provider?
- Do you believe that He is faithful?
- Do you believe that there is more than enough in Him?

Because your answers to those questions will determine how you live.

Overflow is not about excess—it is about trust. It is the confidence that what you release is not your source. That what you give does not diminish you, because your supply is not limited to what is in your hand. When you live from that place, generosity becomes natural.

Breaking the Spirit of Scarcity

One of the greatest enemies of generosity is scarcity. Scarcity is not just a financial condition—it is a mindset.

- It says, "There is not enough."

- It says, "If I give, I will lose."
- It says, "I must protect what I have."

And this mindset affects everything.

- It affects how you give.
- It affects how you relate.
- It affects how you trust God.

Scarcity causes you to hold back. You hold back your resources. You hold back your time. You hold back your encouragement. You hold back your love. Because you are afraid that if you release something, you will not have enough left. But this is not how the Kingdom operates.

The Kingdom is not built on scarcity—it is built on abundance. Not because resources are unlimited in the natural, but because God is unlimited in His provision. When you break agreement with scarcity, something shifts. You begin to see differently. You begin to trust differently. You begin to live differently. You realize that you are not the source—God is. And when God is your source, you are free to give.

Mammon and the Battle for Your Trust

Jesus spoke directly about money in a way that reveals something deeper than finances—He revealed a spiritual battle. He said you cannot serve both God and mammon. Mammon is more than money—it is a system, a spirit, a way of thinking that promises security apart from God. It tells you that your safety is found in what you have, not in who God is.

- Mammon says, "Trust in resources."
- God says, "Trust in Me."
- Mammon says, "Hold tightly."

- God says, "Give freely."
- Mammon says, "Protect yourself."
- God says, "I am your provider."

This is why generosity is not just practical—it is spiritual. Every time you choose to give, you are making a statement about where your trust lies. You are saying, "My security is not in what I have—it is in who God is." And this breaks the hold of mammon. Because mammon loses its power when you stop trusting it.

Generosity as Identity, Not Obligation

One of the biggest misconceptions about generosity is that it is something you are required to do instead of something you are called to become. When generosity is reduced to obligation, it becomes heavy. It feels like something you have to do rather than something you want to do. And anything rooted in obligation will eventually lose joy.

But generosity in the Kingdom is not about obligation—it is about identity. You give because you are like Him. You give because it is who you are becoming. This changes everything. You are not trying to meet a requirement—you are expressing a nature. And when generosity becomes part of your identity, it extends beyond finances. You become generous with your time. Generous with your attention. Generous with your encouragement. Generous with your forgiveness. It becomes a way of living.

Living Open-Handed

Generosity is ultimately about living open-handed. A closed hand cannot receive. When you hold tightly to what you have, you may feel secure, but you limit both what you can give and what you can receive. But when you live open-handed, something shifts. You trust God more. You release more. You receive more.

This is not a formula—it is a posture. It is living with the understanding that everything you have is from Him, and everything you have is meant to flow through you. You are not an owner—you are a steward. And when you live as a steward, you stop clinging and start releasing.

Generosity in Every Area

True generosity is not limited to finances—it touches every part of your life. It shows up in how you treat people. In how you give your time. In how you use your words. In how you respond to need. You can be financially generous but relationally closed. You can give resources but withhold love.

But Kingdom generosity is holistic. It is a lifestyle. It means you are not constantly calculating what something will cost you—you are looking for opportunities to give. To give encouragement. To give kindness. To give support. To give what you carry. Because you realize that what you have is not just for you.

The Joy of Giving

There is a joy that comes with generosity that cannot be found any other way. It is not the joy of gaining—it is the joy of releasing. Because when you give, you align yourself with God's nature. You step into His way of living. And something happens within you. Your grip loosens. Your trust deepens. Your perspective shifts. You begin to realize that life is not about accumulation—it is about impact.

A Life That Reflects Heaven

Heaven is not a place of lack—it is a place of abundance. And when you live from Heaven's culture, your life begins to reflect that. Not necessarily in excess, but in overflow. Where what you have is enough, and what flows from you impacts others. This is what generosity produces. Not just giving—but transformation.

You were created to reflect a generous God. To live open-handed. To trust fully. Not from lack—but from overflow. This is Kingdom culture. And this is what it means to live generously.

Reflection Questions

1. Do I truly see God as my provider, or do my habits and decisions reveal a mindset of scarcity and self-protection?
2. In what areas of my life am I holding tightly instead of living open-handed—whether with finances, time, relationships, or opportunities?
3. What is one intentional act of generosity I can take this week that reflects trust in God and a lifestyle of overflow?

9

UNITY — PROTECTING WHAT GOD BLESSES

WHERE UNITY EXISTS, GOD COMMANDS BLESSING

Unity is not just a good idea—it is a divine environment. There are many things God responds to, but there is something unique about unity. Scripture reveals that where unity is present, God commands blessing. Not suggests it. Not considers it. Commands it.

This means unity is not optional in the Kingdom—it is foundational. If you want to see God move in a sustained way, unity must be present. If you want to see His hand rest on a people, unity must be protected. If you want to build something that lasts, unity must be prioritized.

Because unity creates an environment where God is welcome. It creates alignment. It creates agreement. It creates space for Heaven to move. But unity is not automatic—it must be cultivated and guarded.

The Power of Agreement

Unity is not simply being in the same place—it is being aligned in heart. It is not proximity—it is agreement. You can have people gathered together and still not have unity. You can have structure, systems, and shared activity, but if there is no alignment of heart, unity is absent.

True unity is relational and spiritual. It is people moving together with shared vision, shared values, and shared commitment. It is people choosing to stay connected even when it is not easy. It is people protecting relationship over preference.

Unity carries power. When people are aligned, something begins to multiply. Prayer becomes stronger. vision becomes clearer. impact becomes greater. What one person could not do alone becomes possible together. This is why the early Church moved with such authority. They were not just gathered—they were united. And where unity exists, Heaven responds.

Division Destroys What God Builds

If unity creates an environment for blessing, division creates an environment for breakdown. Division is one of the primary strategies of the enemy. Because he understands something—he does not need to destroy people if he can divide them. He does not need to stop a movement externally if he can fracture it internally.

Division weakens what unity strengthens. It disrupts alignment. It erodes trust. It fractures relationships. And once division takes root, everything begins to suffer. Vision becomes clouded. Momentum slows. People withdraw. What was once strong becomes unstable.

This is why division must be taken seriously. Not ignored. Not tolerated. But addressed. Because what you allow will eventually grow.

The Root of Division: Offense

At the root of most division is offense. Offense is subtle, but it is powerful. It often begins with something small—miscommunication, misunderstanding, unmet expectations, or perceived wrongs. But if it is not addressed, it begins to grow. It shifts your perspective. It changes how you see people. It begins to justify distance.

Offense causes you to focus on what is wrong instead of what is right. It magnifies flaws and minimizes value. It builds a case in your mind that separates you from others. And over time, what began as a moment becomes a mindset.

This is why offense must be confronted quickly. Not externally first—but internally. You must deal with your heart. Because if you allow offense to remain, it will eventually express itself. Through words. Through actions. Through distance. And once it is expressed, division follows.

Gossip: The Language of Division

One of the primary ways division spreads is through gossip. Gossip is not just talking about someone—it is talking about someone in a way that erodes honor, trust, and unity. It often feels justified. You may feel like you are just sharing. Just processing. Just explaining. But if it is not rooted in honor, it becomes destructive.

Gossip spreads perspective. It pulls others into your offense. It creates agreement around negativity. It multiplies division. And what started in one heart begins to affect many. This is why gossip is so dangerous. It rarely feels like division—but it produces it. It rarely feels serious—but it spreads quickly. And once it spreads, it becomes difficult to contain.

Unity requires you to guard your words. Not just what you say to people—but what you say about them. Because your words carry influence.

Disconnection: The Silent Divider

Not all division is loud. Sometimes it is quiet. It looks like disconnection. Pulling back. Withdrawing. Creating distance without addressing the issue. This is one of the most common responses to offense. Instead of leaning in, people step back. Instead of addressing, they avoid. Instead of pursuing, they disconnect. And while this may feel easier in the moment, it creates long-term damage.

Because disconnection does not resolve issues—it deepens them. It allows assumptions to grow. It prevents understanding. It reinforces separation. Unity requires engagement. It requires you to move toward, not away.

Confronting for the Sake of Unity

Unity is not maintained by avoiding issues—it is maintained by addressing them correctly. This is where many people struggle. They either avoid confrontation entirely, or they confront without honor. But Kingdom confrontation is different.

It is not about winning—it is about restoring. It is not about proving a point—it is about protecting relationship. It is not about releasing frustration—it is about bringing clarity. When you confront with the goal of unity, your posture changes. You approach with humility. You speak with honor. You listen with openness.

You seek understanding, not just expression. And in doing so, you create space for resolution. Because most conflict is not about intent—it is about perception. And when people are willing to communicate, much can be restored.

Unity Without Uniformity

One of the misunderstandings about unity is that it requires sameness. But unity is not uniformity. God did not create people to be identical—He created them to be diverse. Different gifts, different personalities, different perspectives. And this diversity is not a problem—it is a strength.

Unity is not about eliminating differences—it is about aligning in the midst of them. You can think differently and still be unified. You can see things differently and still be connected. Because unity is not built on agreement in everything—it is built on commitment to something greater. Shared values. Shared vision. Shared relationship.

This allows for diversity without division. Because the focus is not on being the same—it is on staying connected.

Protecting Unity Intentionally

Unity does not sustain itself. It must be protected. This requires awareness. You must be aware of what threatens it. You must be aware of your own heart. You must be aware of how you respond. You protect unity by dealing with offense quickly. By refusing to engage in gossip. By choosing to pursue relationship instead of withdrawing. By speaking with honor even when it is difficult. You protect unity by valuing it. Because what you value, you guard.

The Cost and Reward of Unity

Unity is not always easy. It requires humility. It requires

patience. It requires forgiveness. It requires choosing relationship over preference. But the reward is worth it. Because where unity exists, God moves. He commands blessing. He releases favor. He establishes what cannot be easily shaken.

Unity creates strength. Not just externally—but internally. It builds resilience. It creates stability. It allows something lasting to be formed.

A People Who Walk in Unity

When a group of people chooses unity, something powerful happens. They become a place where Heaven rests. Not because they are perfect—but because they are aligned. They deal with issues. They protect relationships. They stay connected. And because of that, God entrusts them with more. More presence. More influence. More impact.

You were not created to live divided. You were created to live connected. To build together. To grow together. To walk together. Unity is not just something to pursue. It is something to protect. This is Kingdom culture. And this is how we protect what God blesses.

Reflection Questions

1. Is there any offense, unresolved tension, or disconnection in my relationships that I need to address in order to protect unity?
2. Do my words—especially when others are not present—build unity or subtly create division through gossip or negativity?
3. When conflict arises, do I fight to be right or do I fight for connection, and what would it look like to choose unity in my next response?

10

HUNGER — THE ENGINE OF REVIVAL

THE DIFFERENCE BETWEEN WANTING AND HUNGERING

There is a profound difference between wanting God and being hungry for Him, and that difference defines the depth of a person's spiritual life. Many people want God in a general sense. They believe in Him, they appreciate Him, and they are open to Him being part of their lives. But hunger is something deeper, something weightier. Hunger is not passive or occasional—it is active, intentional, and consuming. It is the internal fire that refuses to let a person settle for surface-level Christianity. Wanting God allows Him to remain an addition to your life, but hunger makes Him essential. It shifts Him from being one priority among many to being the center that everything else revolves around.

Hunger moves you in ways that desire alone cannot. It causes you to pursue when others remain comfortable. It drives you to press in when others pull back. It creates a sense of urgency that cannot be ignored. When you are hungry, you do not need to be reminded to seek God—you feel the necessity of it. You are not satisfied with knowing about Him; you want to encounter Him. You are not content with past experiences; you long for present reality. In the Kingdom, transformation does not come to those who merely desire—it comes to those who pursue. Hunger is what turns belief into action and curiosity into encounter.

Hunger Is a Spiritual Discipline

One of the greatest misunderstandings about hunger is that it is something you either have or do not have based on how you feel. But hunger is not merely an emotion—it is a discipline that must be cultivated. Just like in the natural, where appetite can be trained, strengthened, or diminished, spiritual hunger is shaped by what you feed it. If you wait until you feel hungry to pursue God, you will often find yourself drifting. But if you choose to pursue Him intentionally, even when your emotions are not fully engaged, something begins to awaken within you.

There is a Kingdom principle at work here: hunger grows when it is exercised. The more you seek God, the more you desire Him. The more you encounter His presence, the more you become aware of how much more there is to experience. This is why consistent engagement matters. Time in prayer, worship, and the Word is not about maintaining a routine—it is about cultivating hunger. What begins as discipline eventually becomes delight. What starts as intentional pursuit becomes a natural overflow of desire. Hunger is not something you wait for—it is something you build.

God Responds to Hunger, Not Perfection

Throughout Scripture, one truth remains consistent—God responds to hunger. He is not drawn to perfection, performance, or religious activity. He is drawn to those who seek Him with sincerity and desperation. Hunger creates a posture of dependency, and dependency creates room for relationship. When you are hungry, you are aware of your need. You recognize that you cannot sustain yourself spiritually, emotionally, or even practically without Him. This awareness draws you closer to Him, not out of obligation, but out of necessity.

Hunger positions you for encounter because it opens your heart. It shifts your focus from what is temporary to what is eternal. It moves you beyond surface-level engagement into deeper relationship. When you are hungry, you are not satisfied with occasional moments of connection—you want continual communion. You want to hear His voice, feel His presence, and walk in alignment with His will. God is not withholding Himself from people—He is responding to those who pursue Him. Hunger is what aligns you with that response.

The Subtle Danger of Comfort

One of the greatest enemies of hunger is not opposition—it is comfort. Comfort in itself is not wrong, but it becomes dangerous when it replaces pursuit. When life is stable, when prayers are answered, and when there is no immediate sense of need, it becomes easy to drift into complacency. Complacency rarely announces itself loudly. It creeps in quietly. It shows up in small compromises—less time in prayer, less intentionality in worship, less focus on God's presence.

Over time, the fire that once burned begins to dim, not because God has moved, but because pursuit has lessened. This is what makes complacency so deceptive—it feels normal. It feels manageable. It does not feel like rebellion, but it produces the same result: distance. In the Kingdom, you are either moving forward in pursuit or drifting into passivity. There is no neutral ground. And if hunger is not intentionally cultivated, it will slowly fade under the weight of comfort.

Guarding Against Complacency

Because of this, hunger must be guarded intentionally. You cannot assume it will remain—you must protect it. This requires awareness and honesty. You must be willing to examine your own heart and recognize when your pursuit is becoming routine or when your passion is being replaced by passivity. This is not about condemnation; it is about alignment. It is about staying aware of where you are so you can respond appropriately.

When you recognize complacency, the response is not guilt—it is re-engagement. You return to pursuit. You make space for God again. You intentionally prioritize His presence in your life. Hunger can always be reignited, but it requires a decision. It requires you to choose pursuit over comfort, presence over distraction, and depth over convenience. Guarding hunger is not a one-time decision—it is a continual commitment.

Hunger and the Presence of God

Hunger and the presence of God are inseparable. You cannot sustain hunger without encountering His presence, and you cannot experience His presence deeply without hunger. They feed one another. Hunger draws you into His presence, and His presence increases your hunger. When you truly encounter God—not in a distant or surface-level way, but in a real and personal way—you begin to realize that there is infinitely more to know, to experience, and to walk in.

This realization fuels deeper pursuit. It creates a rhythm in your life where you continually seek, encounter, and hunger for more. This is how spiritual life is meant to function—not as occasional moments of connection, but as an ongoing journey deeper into God. Hunger is not meant to be satisfied once—it is meant to continually grow as you encounter Him.

Living with Continual Pursuit

Hunger is not meant to be seasonal—it is meant to be a lifestyle. It is not confined to specific moments or environments; it is something you carry with you. It shapes how you live, how you think, and how you prioritize your life. When you live with hunger, you become intentional with your time, your attention, and your focus. You begin to structure your life around what matters most—your relationship with God.

This does not mean you are always in an emotional high, but it does mean you are always engaged. Your heart remains open, your spirit remains responsive, and your life remains aligned with pursuit. You are not coasting—you are pressing in. You are not settling—you are seeking. This kind of life creates consistency, depth, and spiritual momentum.

The Cost and Reward of Hunger

Hunger will cost you something. It will require you to make sacrifices. You will have to give up time, comfort, and distractions in order to pursue God fully. You will have to choose presence over convenience and depth over ease. But the cost of hunger is always worth it, because what you gain far outweighs what you give up.

When you pursue God, you gain clarity, strength, and intimacy. You gain a deeper understanding of who He is and who you are in Him. You gain alignment with His will and access to His presence. Most importantly, you gain Him. There is no greater reward than that. The cost of hunger is temporary, but the reward is eternal.

Hunger Produces Fire

When hunger is sustained, it produces something powerful—it produces fire. Not temporary excitement or emotional hype, but a steady, burning passion for God. A life marked by devotion, intensity, and consistency. This is the kind of life that fuels revival. Revival is not built on events or programs—it is built on people who are hungry. People who refuse to settle. People who continue to pursue God regardless of circumstances.

God responds to hunger because hunger creates space for Him to move. It invites His presence, His power, and His purpose. And when a group of people carries this kind of hunger together, it creates an environment where revival is not just possible—it becomes inevitable.

A Life That Burns

At the end of everything, the question is not simply whether you believe in God, but whether your life burns with hunger for Him. Whether you are still pursuing, still seeking, still pressing in. Because a life that is hungry will never be stagnant. It will continue to grow, deepen, and encounter God in new ways.

You were not created to live a passive or comfortable spiritual life. You were created to pursue. You were created to hunger. You were created to press into the fullness of what God has made available. Hunger is the engine that drives your spiritual life forward. It keeps you moving, keeps you seeking, and keeps you aligned with the heart of God. This is Kingdom culture. And this is what fuels revival.

Reflection Questions

1. Would I honestly describe my current walk with God as hungry or comfortable, and what does my daily life reveal about that?
2. What distractions or patterns have been dulling my hunger for God, and what intentional changes do I need to make to pursue Him more deeply?
3. What is one practical way I can increase my pursuit of God this week, even if I don't feel it, to cultivate greater hunger?

11

LEGACY — BUILDING BEYOND YOURSELF

A LIFE THAT OUTLIVES YOU

There is a way to live that is centered entirely on the present, and there is a way to live that is anchored in eternity. One is focused on moments, experiences, and immediate outcomes. The other is focused on legacy—on what remains long after you are gone. The Kingdom of God invites you into the second.

Many people live for what they can see, what they can feel, and what they can accomplish within their own lifetime. They measure success by what they build, what they achieve, and what they experience. But Heaven measures differently. Heaven looks at what continues. It looks at what is multiplied. It looks at what is carried forward into the next generation. Legacy is not about what you accomplish—it is about what you reproduce.

You can build something impressive in your lifetime and still leave nothing behind. You can gather people, create moments, and establish systems, but if those things are not transferred, they will not continue. Legacy requires more than impact—it requires multiplication. This is the shift from living for yourself to living beyond yourself.

Thinking in Generations, Not Moments

One of the defining characteristics of Kingdom culture is generational thinking. God does not think in terms of moments —He thinks in terms of generations. His promises are spoken generationally. His covenant is established generationally. His purposes unfold generationally.

This means that if you are going to align with Him, you must begin to think the same way. You must lift your perspective beyond immediate outcomes and begin to consider what your life is producing over time. You must ask not only, "What am I building?" but "What will remain?" Not only, "What am I doing?" but "Who am I raising?"

Because what you build may impact a moment, but who you raise will impact generations. This changes your priorities. You begin to invest differently. You begin to lead differently. You begin to measure success differently. You are no longer satisfied with temporary results—you want lasting fruit.

Spiritual Multiplication

The Kingdom was never designed for addition—it was designed for multiplication. Addition gathers. Multiplication reproduces. You can add people to something without ever multiplying what is inside of you. But multiplication requires intentional investment. It requires you to take what you carry and deposit it into others in a way that it becomes theirs.

This is how the Kingdom expands. Not just through gatherings, but through people who reproduce what they have received. Jesus modeled this. He ministered to the crowds, but He invested deeply in a few. He did not just teach them—He walked with them. He did not just give them information—He imparted identity, authority, and purpose. And when He was no longer physically present, they continued what He started. This is multiplication. It is not about how many people you reach—it is about how many people you raise. Because what you raise will continue.

Raising Sons and Daughters

At the heart of Kingdom legacy is sonship. God is not building an organization—He is raising a family. He is not looking for followers who remain dependent—He is raising sons and daughters who mature, grow, and eventually become fathers and mothers themselves.

This is the cycle of the Kingdom. Sons become fathers. Daughters become mothers. And what was received is reproduced. Raising sons and daughters requires more than teaching—it requires relationship. It requires time. It requires investment. It requires intentionality. You are not just passing on knowledge—you are shaping identity. You are helping people understand who they are. You are helping them walk in their calling. You are helping them develop the character to sustain what God gives them. This is not quick work. It is slow. It is relational. It is costly. But it is the only way to build something that lasts.

The Responsibility of Spiritual Fathers and Mothers

There comes a point in your journey where your focus must shift. You move from receiving to reproducing. This is where maturity is revealed. It is no longer just about your growth—it is about who you are growing. Spiritual fathers and mothers carry responsibility. They do not just lead—they cover. They do not just instruct—they invest. They do not just direct—they develop.

They take ownership of the people God has entrusted to

them. They see beyond where someone is and begin to invest into who they are becoming. This requires patience. Because people do not grow overnight. It requires wisdom. Because each person is different. It requires love. Because without love, investment becomes obligation. But when done correctly, it produces something powerful. People who are not just followers, but leaders. People who are not just consumers, but builders. People who carry the same DNA and reproduce it in others.

Living for What You May Never See

One of the most powerful aspects of legacy is that you may not see the full result of what you build. This requires a different kind of mindset. You must be willing to invest in what will benefit others more than yourself. You must be willing to sow seeds that will be harvested in a future you may not fully experience.

This is how the Kingdom works. You plant. You water. God brings the increase. And often, that increase extends beyond your lifetime. This requires trust. Trust that what you are building matters. Trust that what you are investing will continue. Trust that God is faithful to complete what He starts. When you live this way, your life becomes less about recognition and more about impact. Less about being seen and more about what remains.

Breaking a Self-Centered Mindset

Legacy requires you to break free from a self-centered mindset. This does not mean you ignore your life—it means you expand your perspective. You begin to see your life as part of something bigger. Your time is not just for you. Your resources are not just for you. Your calling is not just for you. It is meant to flow through you. This is where generosity, family, and leadership all connect. Because when you live beyond yourself, everything begins to multiply.

The Power of Reproduction

Reproduction is the evidence of maturity. If something is healthy, it reproduces. This is true naturally, and it is true spiritually. When you are growing, you should also be helping others grow. When you are being discipled, you should also be discipling. When you are being poured into, you should also be pouring out.

This does not require perfection—it requires participation. You do not have to know everything to invest in someone. You simply have to be willing to share what you have received. And as you do, something begins to multiply. What was once in you begins to exist in others.

Building What Lasts

There are many things you can build in your lifetime. You can build influence. You can build success. You can build systems. But the only thing that truly lasts is people. Everything else fades. But people carry what you give them. They carry your values. They carry your perspective. They carry your investment. And they pass it on. This is how legacy is formed. Not through what you accumulate, but through what you impart.

A Life That Multiplies

When you begin to live with legacy in mind, your life changes. You become more intentional. More focused. More invested. You begin to see every relationship as an opportunity. Every moment as a seed. Every conversation as a chance to build something that will outlast you. You stop living randomly and start living purposefully.

Because you realize that your life is not just about you—it is about what flows through you. You were not created just to live—

you were created to multiply. To build beyond yourself. To raise others. To leave something that remains. This is Kingdom culture. And this is how we build for generations.

Reflection Questions

1. Am I living primarily for what impacts me now, or am I intentionally investing in what will outlive me and impact future generations?
2. Who am I actively pouring into right now, and how am I helping raise others into maturity and leadership?
3. What would it look like for me to shift from adding to something to multiplying what God has placed in me?

12

IDENTITY AND SONSHIP

THE FOUNDATION OF THE KINGDOM LIFE

Everything in the Kingdom begins with identity. Not gifting. Not calling. Not responsibility. Identity. If identity is unclear, everything else becomes unstable. You can have the right theology, the right opportunities, and even the right environment, but if you do not know who you are, you will struggle to live in what God has given you. You will constantly feel like you are trying to become something instead of living from something.

This is where many believers find themselves. They love God, they desire to grow, but internally they are striving. They are trying to earn what has already been given. They are trying to prove what has already been established. They are trying to secure what has already been declared.

And the reason is simple—they do not fully understand their identity. Because identity is not something you create—it is something you receive.

From Orphan Mindset to Sonship

At the core of identity is the difference between an orphan

mindset and a sonship mindset. This is not about natural upbringing—it is about internal perspective.

An orphan mindset is shaped by separation, insecurity, and self-reliance. It believes it must earn love, fight for position, and protect itself from rejection. It measures value based on performance and constantly looks for validation. Even in the Kingdom, people can live with an orphan mindset.

- They can serve God but still feel distant from Him.
- They can work hard but still feel unaccepted.
- They can pursue purpose but still feel insecure.

Because internally, they do not see themselves as sons and daughters—they see themselves as servants trying to earn a place. But sonship is different. Sonship is rooted in relationship, not performance. It is built on the reality that you are already accepted, already loved, already chosen. It is not something you achieve—it is something you step into.

A son does not wake up trying to earn a place in the family. A son lives from the reality that he already belongs. This is the shift. From striving to rest. From earning to receiving. From insecurity to confidence. And until this shift happens, you will always feel like you are trying to prove something instead of living from something.

Identity Shapes Behavior

One of the most important truths to understand is that behavior flows from identity. You do not live differently by trying harder—you live differently by seeing yourself differently. If you see yourself as rejected, you will live guarded. If you see yourself as unworthy, you will live insecure. If you see yourself as alone, you will live independent.

But when your identity shifts, your behavior follows. When you see yourself as loved, you begin to love differently. When you see yourself as accepted, you begin to live confidently. When you see yourself as a son or daughter, you begin to walk in alignment.

This is why transformation must begin with identity. You cannot fix behavior at the surface level and expect lasting change. You must go to the root. And the root is always what you believe about who you are.

Living from Acceptance, Not for It

One of the greatest traps people fall into is living for acceptance instead of from it. Living for acceptance creates pressure. You feel like you have to perform. You feel like you have to prove yourself. You feel like you have to maintain an image. And this leads to exhaustion.

Because you are constantly trying to earn something that has already been given. But the Kingdom invites you into a different way of living. Living from acceptance.

This means you begin from a place of being loved, not trying to be loved. You begin from a place of being secure, not trying to become secure. You begin from a place of being chosen, not trying to be chosen.

This changes everything. You stop striving. You stop comparing. You stop needing validation from others. Because your identity is settled. And when your identity is settled, your life becomes stable.

The Voice That Shapes Identity

Identity is formed by what you listen to. The voice you believe will determine how you see yourself. If you listen to the voice of the world, your identity will be shaped by performance, comparison, and achievement. If you listen to the voice of your past, your identity will be shaped by wounds, failures, and experiences.

But if you listen to the voice of the Father, your identity will be shaped by truth. And His voice is clear. You are loved. You are chosen. You are accepted. You belong. This is not based on what you have done—it is based on what Jesus has done. And when you begin to align with that voice, your identity becomes rooted.

Authority Flows from Identity

In the Kingdom, authority is not something you strive for—it is something you carry. And it flows directly from identity. If you do not know who you are, you will not walk in authority. You will hesitate. You will question. You will doubt.

But when identity is established, authority becomes natural. Because authority is not about position—it is about alignment. A son understands what belongs to him. A son understands his place. A son understands his authority.

This is why Jesus operated with such clarity. He knew who He was. And because of that, He spoke with authority, acted with authority, and lived with authority. Not because He was trying to prove something, but because He was aligned with who He was. And this is what sonship produces.

Breaking the Need for Approval

One of the greatest signs of an orphan mindset is the need for approval. You look to people to affirm you. You look to outcomes to validate you. You look to success to define you. But this creates instability. Because people's opinions change. Outcomes fluctuate. Success is temporary.

If your identity is tied to those things, you will constantly feel unsettled. But when your identity is rooted in sonship, you are free. You no longer need approval to feel secure. You no longer need recognition to feel valuable. You are already established. And from that place, you can live freely.

Becoming Who You Already Are

One of the paradoxes of the Kingdom is that you are becoming who you already are. You are already a son or daughter. But you are growing into the fullness of that reality. This is the process of transformation. It is not becoming something new—it is stepping into what has already been established. And this takes time. It takes renewing your mind. It takes aligning your thoughts. It takes rejecting lies and embracing truth.

But as you do, something begins to shift. You begin to think differently. You begin to respond differently. You begin to live differently. Because your identity is no longer external—it is internal.

A Life Rooted in Sonship

When identity is established, everything else becomes aligned. You love from security. You lead from confidence. You give from abundance. You pursue from rest. Because you are no longer trying to become—you are living from who you are.

This is what makes the Kingdom life sustainable. It is not built on effort—it is built on identity. You were never meant to live as an orphan. You were created to live as a son or daughter. To know who you are. To live from that reality. To carry that identity into everything you do. This is Kingdom culture. And this is where everything begins.

Reflection Questions

1. Do I live from a place of sonship or from an orphan mindset, and what patterns in my life reveal that?
2. In what areas am I striving for acceptance instead of living from the reality that I am already loved and chosen by God?
3. How would my decisions, confidence, and relationships change if I fully embraced my identity as a son or daughter of God?

13 KINGDOM ORDER AND AUTHORITY

GOD BUILDS WITH DESIGN, NOT DISORDER

The Kingdom of God is not random—it is intentional. Everything God builds carries design, structure, and order. From creation itself to the way He establishes His people, there is a pattern to how He moves. He does not build chaotically. He does not release without structure. He does not empower without alignment.

This is important to understand because many people love the power of God but resist the order of God. They want freedom without structure, influence without accountability, and authority without alignment. But in the Kingdom, power and order are not in conflict—they work together.

Order is what sustains what God releases. Without order, what is built becomes unstable. What begins in strength eventually breaks down because it lacks the structure to support it. This is true in every area of life. It is true in families, in churches, in leadership, and in personal growth.

God's design is not restrictive—it is protective. It is not meant to limit you—it is meant to position you. When you understand this, you begin to see order differently. You stop resisting it and start aligning with it. You realize that structure is not something to avoid—it is something to embrace. Because what God builds, He builds with intention.

Alignment Is the Key to Flow

In the Kingdom, alignment determines flow. When something is aligned, it functions properly. It carries what it was designed to carry. It moves with clarity, strength, and consistency. But when something is out of alignment, it creates resistance. It becomes strained. It loses effectiveness.

This is true spiritually as well. When your life is aligned with God, there is flow. His presence flows. His direction becomes clear. His authority rests on you. But when you are out of alignment, things feel difficult.

You may still be active, but there is resistance. You may still be moving, but there is frustration. This is not because God has left—it is because alignment has shifted. This is why order matters. Order brings alignment. Alignment brings flow. And flow allows you to walk in what God has designed for you.

Understanding Authority Correctly

Authority is one of the most misunderstood concepts in the Kingdom. Because of past experiences, abuse, or cultural perspectives, many people associate authority with control, manipulation, or limitation. They see it as something negative—something to resist or avoid.

But true authority in the Kingdom is not about control—it is about responsibility. Authority is given to serve, not to dominate. It is given to protect, not to restrict. It is given to build, not to elevate self. When authority is expressed correctly, it creates life. It brings clarity. It establishes direction. It provides covering.

But when authority is distorted, it becomes harmful. This is why it is so important to understand the difference. Because rejecting authority altogether is not the answer—it leads to independence, which is just as dangerous as control. The goal is not to avoid authority—it is to restore it to its proper design.

Authority vs Control

Control and authority may look similar on the surface, but they come from completely different places. Control is rooted in insecurity. It needs to dominate. It needs to manipulate. It needs to maintain power. Control is self-focused. It is driven by fear, pride, or the need to protect position.

Authority, on the other hand, is rooted in identity and responsibility. It does not need to force—it leads. It does not need to manipulate—it guides. It does not need to protect itself—it protects others. Authority is others-focused. It is given by God and stewarded with humility. This is why true authority carries peace, not pressure. When you are under healthy authority, you feel safe, not restricted. You feel supported, not controlled. You feel strengthened, not diminished. And when you operate in authority correctly, others experience the same.

Submission as Protection

Submission is one of the most misunderstood words in the Kingdom. For many, it carries negative connotations. It feels like loss of control, loss of voice, or loss of freedom. But this is not how God designed it. Submission is not about losing—it is about positioning. It is not about being less—it is about being aligned.

Submission places you under covering. And covering provides protection.

Just as in the natural, where structures provide safety and support, spiritual alignment creates stability. It allows you to grow without being exposed to unnecessary harm. It gives you guidance, accountability, and support. Submission is not about blind obedience—it is about trust. Trusting that God has placed structure for your benefit. Trusting that alignment will lead to growth. And when you see submission this way, it becomes freeing instead of limiting.

The Power of Being Under Authority

Before you can walk in authority, you must learn to be under authority. This is a principle of the Kingdom. Authority flows through alignment. If you are not aligned, you will struggle to carry authority effectively. You may try to operate in it, but it will lack weight. It will lack clarity.

But when you are under authority, something happens. You gain perspective. You gain protection. You gain strength. Because you are not operating alone—you are operating in alignment with something greater. This is why even Jesus demonstrated submission. He did not operate independently—He operated in alignment with the Father. And because of that, He walked in authority. This is the pattern.

Building in Divine Order

God does not just build individuals—He builds structures. Families. Communities. Churches. And these structures require order. Divine order is not about rigid systems—it is about alignment with God's design. It means things are positioned correctly. Relationships are healthy. Leadership is clear. Responsibilities are understood. When this happens, there is strength. Things function as they should. Growth becomes sustainable. What is built begins to last. But when order is ignored, things become unstable. Confusion increases. Misalignment spreads. What was once strong begins to weaken. This is why building with order is essential.

Trusting God's Design

At the core of all of this is trust. Do you trust that God's way is better? Do you trust that His design is for your good? Because if you do not, you will resist it. You will try to build your own way. You will avoid alignment. You will operate independently. But when you trust Him, you begin to embrace His design. You begin to align your life with His structure. You begin to value authority correctly. You begin to see order as something that strengthens you. And as you do, something shifts.

A Life of Alignment

When your life is aligned with God's order, everything begins to flow. Your decisions become clearer. Your direction becomes stronger. Your authority becomes more effective. Because you are no longer striving—you are aligned. And alignment produces fruit. Not temporary fruit—but lasting fruit. You were not created to live in disorder. You were created to live aligned. To walk in authority. To build with clarity. To operate in God's design. This is Kingdom culture. And this is how Heaven builds.

Reflection Questions

1. Am I aligned with God's order in my life, or are there areas where I've resisted structure and authority?
2. Do I view submission as protection and positioning, or do I still see it as limitation—and how is that affecting my growth?
3. In what ways can I better steward authority—either by walking in it with humility or by honoring it in others?

14

SPIRIT-LED DISCIPLESHIP

MORE THAN INFORMATION — THE CALL TO TRANSFORMATION

Discipleship in the Kingdom was never meant to be informational—it was always meant to be transformational. For many, discipleship has been reduced to learning. It becomes about gaining knowledge, understanding Scripture, and growing intellectually. While those things are important, they are not the goal. You can learn truth and still not be changed by it. You can understand Scripture and still live outside of its power. You can sit under teaching for years and remain the same internally.

Because information alone does not produce transformation. Transformation happens when truth is not just known, but encountered, embraced, and lived. It happens when what you learn begins to shape how you think, how you respond, and how you live. This is why discipleship must go beyond information. It must reach the heart. The goal is not to create people who know more—the goal is to raise people who become different.

The Model of Jesus

When you look at the life of Jesus, you do not see Him discipling people primarily through lectures. He taught, but He also walked with people. He invited them into relationship. He allowed them to see how He lived, how He responded, how He prayed, and how He moved with the Father. Discipleship was not a class—it was a life shared.

They learned not just by listening, but by observing. Not just by hearing, but by experiencing. They were shaped by proximity, by relationship, and by encounter. This is the model. Discipleship is not something you attend—it is something you enter. It requires connection. It requires presence. It requires investment. Because people are not formed primarily through information—they are formed through relationship and encounter.

Formation Through Relationship

Transformation happens best in the context of relationship. This is where truth becomes real. In relationship, you are known. In relationship, you are seen. In relationship, you are challenged and encouraged. You cannot hide in real discipleship. Your strengths are seen, but so are your weaknesses. Your potential is recognized, but so are the areas that need growth. And this is where real formation happens. Because growth requires exposure. Not exposure for shame, but exposure for healing. Not exposure for rejection, but exposure for alignment.

When you are in relationship, you cannot remain hidden. And what is brought into the light can be transformed. This is why isolation limits growth. You may gain knowledge, but you will struggle to be formed.

Encounter as a Catalyst for Change

While relationship is essential, encounter is equally necessary. You cannot be fully discipled without encountering God personally. No one can experience God for you. No one can replace your personal connection with Him. You must hear His voice. You must experience His presence. You must walk with Him yourself.

This is where many discipleship models fall short. They focus on teaching people about God without leading them into encountering Him. But information without encounter creates distance. You know about Him, but you do not know Him. Encounter changes that. When you encounter God, something shifts internally. Truth becomes real. Identity becomes clear. Direction becomes personal. Encounter is what moves truth from your mind into your life. And this is why Spirit-led discipleship must include both relationship and encounter.

Being Led by the Spirit in Discipleship

True discipleship is not just leader-led—it is Spirit-led. Leaders have a role, but the Holy Spirit is the ultimate guide. He is the one who reveals truth. He is the one who convicts and corrects. He is the one who leads people into transformation. This requires a shift in how discipleship is approached.

Instead of controlling the process, you learn to partner with what the Spirit is doing. Instead of forcing outcomes, you become sensitive to His timing. Instead of relying solely on structure, you allow space for His leading. This does not remove intentionality —it deepens it. Because you are no longer just discipling people based on what you think they need—you are responding to what God is doing in their life. This creates depth.

Raising Mature Believers

The goal of discipleship is maturity. Not dependence. Not control. Not perpetual immaturity. You are not called to raise people who always need you—you are called to raise people who nd, grow, and lead themselves under the guidance of the Spirit. Mature believers are stable. They are not easily shaken. They are not constantly dependent on others for direction. They are grounded in truth and responsive to the Spirit. They can hear God. They can make decisions. They can walk in alignment. This is what discipleship should produce. Not followers who remain dependent, but sons and daughters who become leaders.

The Danger of Dependency

When discipleship is not done correctly, it creates dependency instead of maturity. People begin to rely on leaders instead of the Spirit. They look for direction externally instead of learning to hear God internally. They become comfortable being led but never grow into leading themselves. This limits growth.

Because you cannot fully walk in your calling if you are always dependent on someone else to guide you. This is why discipleship must be designed to release, not retain. It must equip people to walk with God, not just follow people.

Walking With the Spirit in Growth

Growth in the Kingdom is not just about effort—it is about alignment with the Spirit. The Holy Spirit knows exactly what needs to be addressed in your life. He knows what is ready to be healed, what needs to be challenged, and what needs to be strengthened. When you learn to walk with Him, growth becomes more precise. You are not guessing. You are not striving aimlessly. You are responding. This is where sensitivity becomes important. You must learn to recognize His voice. To respond to His prompting. To trust His leading. Because He will lead you into growth in a way that is both effective and personal.

A Process, Not an Event

Discipleship is not an event—it is a process. It takes time. People are not transformed overnight. They grow gradually, step by step, layer by layer. And this requires patience. You must be willing to walk with people through the process. Through success and failure. Through clarity and confusion. Through growth and resistance. Because transformation is not linear—it is relational. And when you commit to the process, you begin to see real fruit.

Becoming and Reproducing

At the end of discipleship is reproduction. You are not just discipled to grow—you are discipled to disciple. What you receive is meant to be given. As you are formed, you begin to form others. As you grow, you begin to help others grow. This is how the Kingdom expands. Not through programs, but through people. People who have been transformed and who carry that transformation into others' lives.

A Life of Ongoing Formation

Discipleship does not end—it continues. You are always growing. Always learning. Always being formed. There is always more. And when you live with this mindset, you remain teachable. You remain hungry. You remain open. Because you understand that formation is ongoing. You were not called to simply learn—you were called to be transformed. To walk with the Spirit. To grow in maturity. To become someone who reflects Christ. This is Kingdom culture. And this is what true discipleship looks like.

Reflection Questions

1. Am I pursuing transformation or just accumulating information, and where is God inviting me to actually change?
2. Who am I walking in real discipleship with—both receiving from and pouring into—and how intentional am I in those relationships?
3. How is the Holy Spirit currently leading my growth, and am I responding to His voice or relying more on external guidance?

15
TRUTH IN LOVE — KINGDOM COMMUNICATION

THE POWER OF WORDS IN THE KINGDOM

Communication is one of the most powerful forces in your life. Every relationship you have is shaped by it. Every environment you are part of is influenced by it. Words build, and words break. Words bring clarity, and words create confusion. Words can heal, and words can wound.

In the Kingdom, communication is not just a practical skill—it is a spiritual responsibility. Because what you say reveals what is in your heart. Jesus made it clear that out of the abundance of the heart, the mouth speaks. This means your words are not random—they are the overflow of what is happening within you. If there is fear in your heart, it will show up in your words. If there is insecurity, it will come out in how you speak. If there is love, truth, and peace, those will be expressed as well.

This is why Kingdom communication is not just about learning what to say—it is about becoming someone whose heart is aligned with truth and love. Because when your heart is healthy, your words will follow.

Truth and Love Must Stay Together

In the Kingdom, truth and love are never meant to be separated. Truth without love becomes harsh. It feels cold, critical, and condemning. It may be accurate, but it lacks the heart that brings transformation. When truth is delivered without love, people often shut down instead of opening up. On the other hand, love without truth becomes weak.

It avoids difficult conversations. It prioritizes comfort over growth. It allows issues to remain unaddressed in the name of maintaining peace. But this kind of love does not actually help people—it leaves them stuck. Kingdom communication holds both together. Truth brings clarity. Love brings connection. Truth says what needs to be said. Love determines how it is said.

When these two come together, something powerful happens. People are able to receive correction without feeling rejected. They are able to grow without feeling condemned. They are able to be challenged while still feeling valued. This is the goal.

Speaking Truth with Grace

Speaking truth is necessary, but how you speak it matters just as much as what you say. Grace is what makes truth receivable. It shapes your tone. It shapes your posture. It shapes your intent. When you speak with grace, you are not trying to prove a point—you are trying to build a person. You are not trying to win an argument—you are trying to strengthen a relationship.

This requires self-awareness. You must check your heart before you speak. Are you speaking from frustration or from love? Are you reacting or responding? Are you trying to release something or resolve something? Because the same truth can either build or break, depending on how it is delivered. Grace slows you down. It helps you choose your words carefully. It reminds you that the goal is not just to be heard—it is to be understood.

Confrontation as Connection

Confrontation is one of the most avoided aspects of communication, but it is also one of the most necessary. Many people see confrontation as conflict. They associate it with tension, discomfort, and division. And because of that, they avoid it. They suppress issues, ignore problems, and hope things will resolve on their own.

But in the Kingdom, confrontation is not meant to divide—it is meant to connect. When done correctly, confrontation strengthens relationships. It brings clarity. It removes misunderstanding. It creates space for growth. Avoiding confrontation does not protect relationships—it weakens them. Unspoken issues create distance. Assumptions replace communication. Frustration builds over time. But when you address things directly, something shifts. You bring things into the light. You create understanding. You restore alignment. Confrontation, when rooted in love, is one of the greatest tools for connection.

Healthy Communication Requires Maturity

Healthy communication does not happen automatically—it requires maturity. It requires you to take responsibility for your words, your tone, and your reactions. It requires you to listen, not just speak. It requires you to be willing to understand, not just to be understood.

Immature communication is reactive. It is driven by emotion. It is defensive. It is focused on self. But mature communication is intentional. It is thoughtful. It is measured. It is focused on relationship. This means you do not say everything you feel in the moment. You process before you respond. You choose your words carefully. You remain aware of how your communication is affecting others. Maturity does not mean you avoid difficult conversations—it means you handle them well.

Breaking Passive Patterns

One of the most common unhealthy communication patterns is passivity. Passive communication avoids confrontation. It suppresses thoughts and feelings. It stays silent when something needs to be said. It prioritizes avoiding tension over addressing truth. This often comes from fear. Fear of rejection. Fear of conflict. Fear of being misunderstood. But passivity creates problems.

What is not addressed does not disappear—it grows. Small issues become larger. Frustration builds internally. Distance increases. Over time, passivity leads to disconnection. Breaking this pattern requires courage. You must be willing to speak. To express. To engage. Not aggressively, but honestly. Because silence does not protect relationships—healthy communication does.

Breaking Aggressive Patterns

On the other side of passivity is aggression. Aggressive communication forces truth without love. It is harsh. It is reactive. It is often driven by emotion rather than clarity. Aggression may feel powerful in the moment, but it damages relationships. It creates defensiveness. It shuts people down. It breaks trust.

Breaking aggressive patterns requires humility. You must learn to slow down. To listen. To respond instead of react. You must learn that being right is not the goal—being effective is. Because if your truth pushes people away, it is not producing what it should.

Becoming a Powerful Person in Communication

In the Kingdom, a powerful person is not someone who controls others—it is someone who is in control of themselves. This is especially true in communication. A powerful person can remain calm in tension. They can listen without becoming defensive. They can speak truth without losing love. They do not allow emotions to dictate their response—they choose their response intentionally. This kind of communication creates safety. People feel heard. People feel valued. People feel understood. And when people feel that, relationships grow stronger.

Listening as an Act of Love

Communication is not just about speaking—it is about listening. Listening communicates value. It shows that you care. It shows that you are present. It shows that you are willing to understand. Many people listen to respond. They are thinking about what they will say next instead of truly hearing what is being said.

But Kingdom communication listens to understand. It creates space. It asks questions. It seeks clarity. Because understanding builds connection.

Building a Culture of Communication

When individuals begin to communicate this way, it creates a culture. A culture where truth is spoken. Where love is felt. Where issues are addressed. Where relationships are strengthened. This kind of culture is not built overnight—it is developed over time. It requires consistency. It requires intentionality. It requires commitment. But the result is powerful. Relationships become healthy. Trust increases. Unity strengthens.

Living It Daily

Kingdom communication is not just for big moments—it is for everyday life. It shows up in small conversations. In how you respond to frustration. In how you handle misunderstanding. It is lived daily.

And over time, it shapes everything. You were created to speak life. To bring clarity. To build relationships. To carry truth and love together. This is Kingdom culture. And this is how we communicate as Heaven's people.

Reflection Questions

1. Do my words consistently reflect both truth and love, or do I tend to lean toward one at the expense of the other?
2. When tension or conflict arises, do I avoid it, react to it, or intentionally engage in a way that strengthens connection?
3. What communication pattern—passive or aggressive—do I need to break, and what would it look like to respond with maturity and grace instead?

16
HOLINESS AND HIDDENNESS

WHAT YOU ARE IN SECRET IS WHO YOU ARE

There is a version of your life that people see, and there is a version of your life that only God sees. One is public. The other is private. One is visible. The other is hidden. And in the Kingdom, it is the hidden life that defines everything.

You can build something externally that looks strong, impactful, and successful, but if your private life is weak, it will eventually be revealed. You can carry influence publicly while lacking integrity privately, but over time, what is hidden will surface. Because in the Kingdom, God does not build from the outside in —He builds from the inside out.

What you are in secret is who you are. Not what you present. Not what you project. Not what others perceive. But who you are when no one is watching. This is where holiness begins. Not in behavior modification for others to see, but in alignment with God in the places no one else can measure. It is in the thoughts you entertain, the decisions you make in private, and the way you steward your heart when there is no audience. This is the foundation of everything.

Private Life Produces Public Power

There is a direct connection between your private life and your public effectiveness. Public power is not sustained by gifting —it is sustained by character. It is not built on moments—it is built on consistency. It is not maintained by appearance—it is upheld by integrity. Many people want influence. They want impact. They want to be used by God in visible ways. But few are willing to cultivate the hidden life that sustains it.

Because the hidden life requires discipline. It requires showing up when no one sees. It requires choosing right when no one would know otherwise. It requires consistency without recognition. But this is where strength is formed. In the quiet place. In the unseen moments. In the decisions that no one applauds. This is where God develops depth. And without depth, influence becomes dangerous.

Holiness Is Alignment, Not Perfection

Holiness is often misunderstood. Some see it as perfection—never making mistakes, never failing, never struggling. Others see it as restriction—a list of rules that limit freedom. But neither of these reflect the true nature of holiness. Holiness is alignment.

It is your life coming into agreement with God's nature, God's truth, and God's ways. It is not about striving to be flawless —it is about consistently turning toward Him, choosing truth over compromise, and living in a way that reflects who He is.

Holiness is relational before it is behavioral. It flows from love, not fear. It flows from identity, not pressure. It flows from connection, not obligation. When you love God, you desire to align with Him. You become aware of what draws you closer to

Him and what pulls you away. And because you value the relationship, you choose alignment. This is holiness.

Purity and Integrity

Two of the key expressions of holiness are purity and integrity. Purity is about what you allow into your life. It is about guarding your heart, your mind, and your spirit. It is being intentional about what you entertain, what you focus on, and what you give access to your inner world. Because what you allow in will shape what comes out.

Integrity is about consistency. It is being the same person in private as you are in public. It is living without hidden contradictions. It is aligning your actions with your values, your words with your life, and your beliefs with your behavior. Integrity creates stability. It removes fragmentation. It removes duplicity. It creates wholeness. And when you live with integrity, your life carries weight.

Living for God, Not for Appearance

One of the greatest challenges in the Christian life is the temptation to live for appearance instead of authenticity. It is easy to build an image. To say the right things. To present yourself in a certain way. But appearance is fragile. It is dependent on perception. It is maintained by performance. It is vulnerable to exposure.

But when you live for God instead of appearance, something shifts. You are no longer focused on how you are seen—you are focused on who you are becoming. You are not trying to impress people—you are aligning with God. This brings freedom. Freedom from comparison. Freedom from pressure. Freedom from needing approval. Because your life is anchored in something deeper than perception.

Consecration: Setting Yourself Apart

Holiness also involves consecration. Consecration is the decision to set yourself apart for God. It is saying, "My life is not my own—I belong to Him." It is choosing to live differently, not out of obligation, but out of devotion. This affects how you live. What you say yes to. What you say no to. How you spend your time. How you steward your life.

Consecration is not about isolation—it is about intentionality. It is not about withdrawing from the world—it is about living in the world with a different standard. And this is what gives your life distinctiveness.

The Power of Hidden Seasons

Not every season of your life will be visible. There will be seasons where you are hidden. Seasons where you are not recognized. Not promoted. Not seen. And these seasons can be difficult if you do not understand their purpose. But hidden seasons are not wasted—they are formative.

This is where God develops character. Where He refines motives. Where He strengthens your foundation. In hidden seasons, you are not being overlooked—you are being prepared. Prepared for what is ahead. Prepared for what you will carry. Prepared for what God will entrust to you. This is where depth is built.

Faithfulness in the Unseen

Faithfulness in the hidden is one of the greatest indicators of maturity. It is easy to be faithful when people are watching. When there is recognition. When there is reward. But true faithfulness is revealed in the unseen. When no one knows. When no one notices. When there is no immediate benefit. This is where your motives are tested. Are you doing this for God, or for recognition? Are you pursuing Him, or pursuing visibility? Because what you do in the hidden will determine what you can carry in the open.

Lasting Fruit Comes from Deep Roots

Anything that produces lasting fruit must have deep roots. And roots are developed in the hidden. They are not visible, but they are essential. They determine stability. They determine strength. They determine sustainability.

If you focus only on what is visible, you may grow quickly, but you will not last. But if you invest in the hidden, you may grow slower, but you will grow stronger. And strength is what sustains fruit.

A Life That Pleases God

At the end of everything, the goal is not to be seen—it is to be known by God. To live a life that pleases Him. Not just publicly, but privately. Not just externally, but internally. To walk in alignment. To live with integrity. To pursue holiness. This is what gives your life weight. You were not created to live for appearance. You were created to live for God. To be whole. To be pure. To be aligned. In the seen and in the unseen. This is Kingdom culture. And this is where true strength is formed.

Reflection Questions

1. Who am I when no one is watching, and does my private life align with the life I present publicly?
2. Are there areas of compromise in my thoughts, habits, or decisions that God is inviting me to bring into alignment with Him?
3. How am I responding to hidden or unseen seasons—am I resisting them or embracing them as preparation for lasting fruit?

17

POWERFUL PEOPLE WHO FIGHT FOR CONNECTION

REDEFINING POWER IN THE KINGDOM

The Kingdom of God redefines what power looks like. In the world, power is often associated with control. It is about influence over others, the ability to dominate, to win, to get your way. It is measured by position, status, and the ability to affect outcomes externally. But in the Kingdom, power is not defined by control over others—it is defined by mastery within yourself.

A powerful person in the Kingdom is not someone who can control others—it is someone who can control their own responses. They are not ruled by emotion. They are not driven by fear. They are not reactive in moments of tension.

Instead, they are steady, anchored, and intentional. They choose how they respond. They choose how they speak. They choose how they engage. This is real power. Because anyone can react—but it takes maturity to respond.

Emotional Maturity in the Kingdom

Emotional maturity is not often talked about in spiritual terms, but it is deeply connected to Kingdom living. You can be spiritually aware but emotionally immature. You can hear God, understand truth, and still struggle in relationships because you have not developed the ability to manage your emotions in a healthy way.

Emotional maturity means you are aware of what you feel, but you are not controlled by it. You can feel frustration without becoming reactive. You can feel hurt without shutting down. You can feel tension without escalating conflict. This does not mean you ignore your emotions—it means you process them. You take them to God. You bring them into the light. You allow truth to shape your response. Emotionally mature people do not deny what they feel—they steward it. And this is essential for healthy relationships.

Taking Ownership of Your Reactions

One of the clearest signs of maturity is ownership. Immaturity blames. Maturity takes responsibility. When something happens, immature thinking says, "They made me feel this way." But mature thinking says, "This is what I am feeling, and I am responsible for how I respond."

This is not about dismissing what others do—it is about recognizing that your response is always your responsibility. No one else controls your reactions. They may influence you. They may trigger something in you. But they do not determine how you respond. And this is where your power is.

Because when you take ownership, you regain control. You are no longer at the mercy of others' behavior. You are no longer reactive. You are intentional. You choose to pause. You choose to process. You choose to respond with truth. This is what it means to be powerful.

Triggers Reveal What Needs Healing

Often, what we call "reactions" are actually indicators of deeper issues. When something triggers you, it is revealing something. It may be a wound. It may be an insecurity. It may be a lie you have believed. And instead of ignoring it or projecting it onto others, maturity allows you to look inward. It asks, "Why did this affect me the way it did?" Because what is triggered is often what needs healing. This is not about blaming yourself—it is about understanding yourself. And when you understand, you can bring those areas to God. You can invite healing. You can replace lies with truth. You can grow. This is how emotional maturity develops.

Fighting for Relationship, Not Control

In moments of tension, you have a choice. You can fight to be right, or you can fight for relationship. You can try to control the outcome, or you can pursue connection. Control focuses on winning. It pushes, it forces, it insists. But connection focuses on relationship. It listens. It understands. It seeks resolution.

When you fight for control, you may win the moment but lose the relationship. But when you fight for connection, you preserve what matters most. This does not mean you avoid truth—it means you approach it differently. You speak truth with love. You confront with humility. You prioritize understanding. Because the goal is not to dominate—it is to restore.

Staying Connected in Tension

Tension is inevitable in relationships. Misunderstandings happen. Expectations are not always met. People make mistakes. But the goal is not to avoid tension—the goal is to remain connected through it. This is what powerful people do. They do not withdraw when things get difficult. They do not shut down when they are hurt. They do not create distance when there is conflict. They lean in. They communicate. They engage. They pursue understanding. Because they value the relationship more than the discomfort.

Refusing to Withdraw

One of the most common responses to tension is withdrawal. It feels safer. You pull back. You disengage. You avoid the situation. But withdrawal creates distance. And distance weakens connection. Powerful people refuse to withdraw. They recognize the impulse, but they choose a different response. They move toward, not away. They address, not avoid. They engage, not disconnect. This is not always easy, but it is necessary. Because relationships cannot grow if they are constantly avoided.

Responding Instead of Reacting

Reaction is immediate. It is driven by emotion. It is often unfiltered. It can escalate situations quickly. Response is intentional. It is thoughtful. It is measured. It brings clarity instead of confusion. Powerful people learn to pause. They do not let the first emotion dictate their response. They take time to process, to think, to align with truth before they speak or act. This pause creates space. Space for wisdom. Space for perspective. Space for love. And in that space, better decisions are made.

Living as a Powerful Person in Love

At the core of all of this is love. Not passive love, but intentional love. Love that chooses connection. Love that values relationship. Love that remains steady even when things are difficult. A powerful person is someone who loves consistently. Not based on how others behave, but based on who they are. They do not withhold love when they are hurt. They do not remove connection when things are hard. They remain. They pursue. They engage. Because love is their foundation.

Creating Safe Relationships

When you live this way, you create safety. People feel safe to be honest. Safe to be known. Safe to grow. Because they know that you will not react unpredictably. They know that you will handle tension with maturity. They know that you will fight for the relationship, not against it. And this kind of environment produces growth. It allows people to open up. To be real. To be transformed.

A Life That Reflects the Kingdom

This is what Kingdom relationships look like. People who are emotionally mature. Who take ownership. Who fight for connection. Who live in love. Not perfect people—but intentional people. People who are growing, learning, and aligning with truth. You were not created to be reactive. You were created to be powerful. To take ownership. To pursue connection. To live in love. This is Kingdom culture. And this is how Heaven's people relate.

Reflection Questions

1. Do I tend to react based on my emotions or respond intentionally, and what does that reveal about my level of emotional maturity?
2. When I feel triggered or hurt, do I take ownership of my response and look inward, or do I place blame on others?
3. In moments of tension, am I fighting for connection or trying to control the outcome—and how can I choose love in my next interaction?

CONCLUSION

BUILDING THE CULTURE OF THE KINGDOM TOGETHER

This Is Not Just a Message — It Is a Mandate

Everything you have just read is not meant to stay on pages—it is meant to become your life. This is not just teaching to be understood. It is not just truth to be agreed with. It is a mandate to be lived out. The Kingdom of God is not advanced through information—it is advanced through people who embody what they believe. It is built by those who do not just hear truth, but who become it.

You were never called to simply believe in the Kingdom—you were called to build it. This means the responsibility is no longer external. It is not just on leaders, churches, or movements. It is on you. It is on every believer who has encountered truth and now carries the responsibility to live it out. Because culture is not created by intention alone—it is created by expression. What you live consistently, you reproduce.

Culture Is a Shared Responsibility

Culture does not exist because someone defines it—it exists

because people live it. It is the invisible environment created by visible behavior. It is what people experience when they are around you. It is what is reinforced through your words, your actions, your priorities, and your responses.

This means culture is not built from the top down—it is built from the inside out and the ground up. Every person contributes. Every interaction matters. Every response reinforces something. Every decision either builds or weakens culture. You are not just influenced by culture—you are influencing it.

This is why you cannot remain passive. If you do not intentionally live Kingdom culture, something else will take its place. And that "something else" will always default to fear, pride, control, or self-centeredness. But when you intentionally live in love, humility, honor, unity, generosity, and truth, you begin to shape an environment. You begin to build something.

Becoming Carriers of Heaven

The goal is not just to understand Heaven—it is to carry it. Heaven is not just a future destination—it is a present reality meant to be expressed through your life. Jesus did not just preach about Heaven—He demonstrated it. He revealed what it looks like when God's nature, power, and presence are made visible on the earth. And now, that same calling rests on you.

You are called to carry Heaven into every environment you step into. Into your home. Into your workplace. Into your relationships. Into your community. This means you do not adapt to every environment—you influence it. You bring peace into chaos. You bring truth into confusion. You bring love into brokenness. Not because you are trying to create something, but because you are carrying something. This is what it means to live as a citizen of Heaven.

The Call to Build, Not Just Believe

Belief without action creates distance. You can agree with truth and still live unchanged. You can acknowledge what is right without ever stepping into it. But the Kingdom is not built on agreement—it is built on participation. You are called to build. To build relationships rooted in honor. To build communities marked by unity. To build lives that reflect holiness and integrity. To build environments where God is welcome.

Building requires intentionality. It requires effort. It requires consistency. It requires commitment. It means you do not wait for someone else to create what you are called to carry. You take responsibility. You begin where you are. You live it out in your daily life. Because every great move of God begins with individuals who choose to live differently.

It Starts with You

It is easy to look at the world and see what needs to change. To see brokenness. To see division. To see dysfunction. But transformation does not begin "out there"—it begins within you. It begins in how you think. In how you respond. In how you live.

You cannot control everything around you, but you can steward what is within you. You can choose love. You can choose humility. You can choose honor. You can choose unity. And as you do, something begins to shift. Not just in your life, but in the lives of those around you. Because transformation is contagious.

Vision: Families, Churches, and Cities Transformed

When Kingdom culture is lived out consistently, it does not stay contained—it expands. It begins in individuals, but it flows into families. Families marked by love instead of dysfunction. By communication instead of silence. By honor instead of division. From families, it flows into communities.

Communities where people are known, supported, and strengthened. Where relationships are real and growth is intentional. From communities, it flows into churches. Churches that are not just gatherings, but families. Not just structured, but alive. Not just informed, but transformed. And from there, it reaches cities.

Because when enough people carry Heaven, environments begin to change. Workplaces shift. Schools shift. Systems shift. Not because of external pressure, but because of internal transformation. This is how the Kingdom advances.

A People Who Reflect Heaven

At the end of everything, the goal is simple. To become a people who reflect Heaven. People who love deeply. Who walk humbly. Who live generously. Who pursue God passionately. Who build with integrity. Who protect unity. Who carry His presence. Not perfectly, but consistently. People who are committed to becoming more like Him in every area of life.

The Invitation

This is the invitation. To not just read this, but to live it. To not just agree with it, but to embody it. To not just be inspired, but to be transformed. To become someone who carries the culture of the Kingdom wherever you go. Because the world does not need more information—it needs demonstration. It needs people who live differently. Who love differently. Who lead differently. People who reflect Heaven. You were created for this. To build. To carry. To transform. Not just in one area—but in every area of your life. This is Kingdom culture. And now, it is yours to live.

Reflection Questions

1. Am I just agreeing with Kingdom culture, or am I actively building it through how I live, lead, and relate to others?
2. In what environments has God placed me to carry His presence and culture, and how intentional am I about influencing those spaces?
3. What is one practical step I can take this week to move from believing the Kingdom to building it in my daily life?

ABOUT THE AUTHOR

Tom Cornell is the Senior Leader of SOZO Church in Washington state, founder of Walk in the Light International and SOZO Network. Tom is married to his beautiful wife Katy and lives in the Puget Sound area with her and their three kids. He has been in ministry pastoring and teaching the body of Christ since 2008.

He has a passion to see the body of Christ moving from people with an orphan mindset to that of sonship; equipping the body to do the work of Jesus resulting in seeing the Kingdom of God manifested here on earth.

www.ingramcontent.com/pod-product-compliance
Lightning Source LLC
LaVergne TN
LVHW010904110826
845149LV00005B/1463

* 9 7 8 1 9 6 9 8 8 2 3 3 3 *